J. 7 J. Ostwalt

Educational Policy
and
International Assessment

THE NATIONAL SOCIETY
FOR THE STUDY OF EDUCATION

Series on Contemporary Educational Issues
Kenneth J. Rehage, Series Editor

The 1975 Titles

Systems of Individualized Education, Harriet Talmage, Editor
Schooling and the Rights of Children, Vernon F. Haubrich and
   Michael W. Apple, Editors
*Educational Policy and International Assessment: Implications of
   the IEA Surveys of Achievement*, Alan C. Purves and Daniel U.
   Levine, Editors

The National Society for the Study of Education also publishes Yearbooks which are distributed by the University of Chicago Press. Inquiries regarding all publications of the Society, as well as inquiries about membership in the Society, may be addressed to the Secretary-Treasurer, 5835 Kimbark Avenue, Chicago, IL 60637. Membership in the Society is open to any who are interested in promoting the investigation and discussion of educational questions.

Educational Policy and International Assessment

IMPLICATIONS OF THE IEA SURVEYS OF ACHIEVEMENT

Edited by

Alan C. Purves
University of Illinois
Urbana

and

Daniel U. Levine
University of Missouri
Kansas City

McCutchan Publishing Corporation
2526 Grove Street
Berkeley, California 94704

379.15
E24

ISBN O-8211-1515-4

Library of Congress Catalog Card Number 74-30962

78-6203

Series Foreword

A most significant undertaking in recent years has been a monumental study based on an international assessment of educational achievement. Findings from that study have thus far appeared in four major volumes, and additional publications are scheduled to appear in the near future. The present volume, consisting of papers and commentaries presented at a conference at the Harvard Graduate School of Education, is designed to provide the general reader with an overview of the results of the study that have thus far been released and their implications for educational policy. A major theme relating to the effects of schooling recurs in many of the papers. Considerable attention is given also to some of the interesting methodological problems that attend a cross-national study of this kind.

Educational Policy and International Assessment is one of four titles in the 1975 Series on Contemporary Educational Issues published under the auspices of the National Society for the Study of Education. Other titles in the series are:

Systems of Individualized Education, edited by Harriet Talmage;
Reading: Some Points of View, edited by Samuel Weintraub;
Schooling and the Rights of Children, edited by Vernon F. Haubrich and Michael W. Apple.

The Society appreciates the efforts of the editors of this volume, Professors Alan C. Purves and Daniel U. Levine, in putting together a most interesting collection of essays.

Kenneth J. Rehage

for the Committee on the Expanded
Publication Program of the
National Society for the Study
of Education

Preface

Since the 1950s a group of researchers affiliated under the title International Association for the Evaluation of Educational Achievement (IEA) has been making a series of international surveys in that field. The Harvard University Graduate School of Education simultaneously became a center for analysis of surveys of educational achievement. It was fitting, therefore, that Harvard and the IEA should join in a stock-taking session, one that would seek to summarize the work of the preceding decades and glance ahead at the future of educational research as an international enterprise. The Harvard-IEA conference, held in November 1973, was such a session. It climaxed fifteen years of educational research.

The conference itself was structured so as to include a variety of types of deliberations. There were presentations on national findings in Japan, Chile, and New Zealand. There were discussions by subject-matter experts on the results of learning in science, the mother tongue, and second languages, and by psychometricians on the methodology of regression analysis. There were informal sessions on problems of cultural pluralism and education in a variety of countries. Plenary sessions were devoted to the major papers, responses to them, and subsequent discussion. The present volume is, then, but the tip of an iceberg. Though the conference was large and was difficult to handle logistically and linguistically, its participants felt, nonetheless, that it was successful, not the least for its demonstration that, as Alan Anderson of Australia wrote: "Notwithstanding the deep involvement of many of the conference participants in the projects themselves the conference was marked by commendable restraint and a readiness to acknowledge important difficulties and limitations which persist in spite of best endeavors."

This volume contains most of the major papers and commentaries of the conference. T. Neville Postlethwaite's contribution sets the stage by summarizing the main findings of the studies in mathematics, science, reading, literature, civic education, French, and English. Since national governments were deeply involved in the project, one result of the studies should be information of use to educational policy planners at both the national and international levels. William J. Platt sets forth some of the issues that such planners must consider and the ways in which the studies of the IEA can and cannot be used to help in the decision-making process. The commentary by Richard J. Light explores some of the technical reasons why such studies cannot be used as the sole source of information for policy decisions and what further kinds of studies and analyses need to be made. The third major paper, by Benjamin S. Bloom, explores the curricular implications of the findings of the IEA; the comments of Endre Ballér and Ralph W. Tyler focus on specific ramifications of Bloom's paper.

One of the major controversies that has arisen from the kind of analysis that the IEA and other recent surveys have used is that pertaining to the relative effects of the children's home background and of the school on the achievement of those children. Robert L. Thorndike discusses the IEA results from this perspective. One major paper, by James S. Coleman, explored the effects of school on learning; it is unfortunate that it is too long for inclusion in this volume. Coleman's thesis is that most models of regression analysis are limited in that they fail to indicate clearly that the home environment and the kind of school a child attends are closely related and that both of these factors can influence the kind of instruction the school provides. But in order to depict the effects of instruction independently of the environment in which the instruction takes place, one needs a more complex statistical model. A reanalysis of the data of the IEA according to such a model indicates that "reading achievement is more fully an outgrowth of home influences than are [science or literature]." Coleman continues: "This is a rather important result, because it indicates that the general finding in this study and others that home background is a much more powerful influence than school influences in determining achievement is a result that is subject specific. . . . It suggests also that the large body of research on relative effects of school and home for learning has focussed on the one performance variable, reading, which may be most dependent on home and least on school, thus understating the effects of school resources when generalized beyond reading." Ronald Edmonds and Sarane Spence Boocock comment on Thorndike's contribution. Marshall S. Smith's commentary, while originally based on Coleman's paper, serves as a further commentary on the issues raised by the general topic of home and school.

One of the major concerns of educational policy makers in Europe has been the selectivity of the educational system. Torsten Husén shows how the findings of the IEA illuminate this concern and, in particular, indicates the usefulness of comparative research in providing a "natural experiment" that can supply evidence to decision makers. J. R. Gass and Martin Trow explore the other social and cultural facets of the question of comprehensive schooling. The final paper, by John Vaizey, explores the findings of the IEA and their relationship to the economics of education, a theme that has been foreshadowed by the papers of Platt and Husén. The paper and commentaries upon it by Jacques Hallak, Angus Maddison, and Russell G. Davis examine alternative theories in the economics of education and alternative interpretations of the findings of the IEA in the light of those theories.

Aside from a spirit of goodwill and this volume, the value of which its readers may judge, what were the results of the conference? First, there was consensus that the claim that "schools don't make a difference" could no longer reasonably be made; the effects of schooling are subtle and multifarious. Second, there was agreement that in analyzing data of the sort the IEA studies produced even the most sophisticated of multiple regression techniques would not suffice, for the relationships among test scores, school, home, teacher, and student variables are complex indeed. The third result was the reexamination of the disclaimer of the IEA concerning an "educational

Olympics." The results of the studies indicate clear discrepancies between the more and less technologically developed nations as well as discrepancies within those groups of nations. These results are also complex because the patterns of national achievement in relation to the achievements of other nations are not simply stated. From the conference came a clear sense that an educational Olympics was a necessary means of allowing policy makers in different countries to examine the educational goals of their countries in light of their own needs and aspirations. In order that such reexamination might take place, the kind of international cooperation that the IEA affords is a necessity.

Many people helped make the conference and this volume possible. The Steering Committee (Paul Ylvisacker, Dean of the Harvard Graduate School of Education, Torsten Husén, Alan C. Purves, and Roy Phillipps, Chairman and Executive Director of IEA) provided the sketch for the conference. The real work of building it, however, fell upon Shirley Isgaard of IEA, Fritz Mosher and Marion Crowley of Harvard, and, particularly, Carol Kolson, also of Harvard, who performed a wide variety of functions. All four helped in the preparation of this manuscript, which has been ably copy edited by Cathy Stevens of the University of Illinois. To all of them and to many others on the IEA, Harvard, and University of Illinois staffs we extend our sincere thanks.

Alan C. Purves
Daniel U. Levine

Contributors

Endre Balle'r, Department of General Education, Ministry for Cultural Affairs, Budapest, Hungary

Benjamin S. Bloom, Charles H. Swift Distinguished Service Professor of Education, University of Chicago

Sarane Spence Boocock, Associate, Russell Sage Foundation, New York City

Russell G. Davis, Professor of Education, Center for Studies in Education and Development, Harvard University

Ronald Edmonds, Center for Urban Studies, Harvard University

J. R. Gass, Director, Center for Educational Research and Innovation, Organization for Economic Cooperation and Development, Paris, France

Jacques Hallak, International Institute for Educational Planning, Paris, France

Torsten Husén, Chairman, International Association for the Evaluation of Educational Achievement, Professor of International Education and Director, Institute for the Study of International Problems in Education, University of Stockholm, Stockholm, Sweden

Richard J. Light, Professor of Statistics and Educational Psychology, Graduate School of Education, Harvard University

Angus Maddison, Center for Educational Research and Innovation, Organization for Economic Cooperation and Development, Paris, France

William J. Platt, Director, Department of Planning and Financing of Education, UNESCO, Paris, France

T. Neville Postlethwaite, International Institute for Educational Planning, Paris, France, and formerly Executive Director, International Association for the Evaluation of Educational Achievement

Marshall S. Smith, Professor of Education, Center for Educational Policy Research, Harvard University

Robert L. Thorndike, Professor of Psychology and Education, Teachers College, Columbia University

Martin Trow, Professor, Graduate School of Public Policy, University of California, Berkeley

Ralph W. Tyler, Science Research Associates, Chicago, Illinois

John Vaizey, Professor of Economics, Brunel University, Uxbridge, England

Contents

1. The Surveys of the International Association for the Evaluation of Educational Achievement (IEA)

T. Neville Postlethwaite

In 1959 educational research centers in twelve countries undertook a pilot project to study educational achievement in reading comprehension, mathematics, science, geography, and nonverbal ability.[1] The target population consisted of all children in the twelve countries whose ages ranged from thirteen years to thirteen years, eleven months, since this was the last age span where practically all of the age group were still in school in all countries. In most cases children in schools or areas that were known to be near the national mean and standard deviation were tested; thus there was no strict probability sample. Tests consisting of a total of 120 items were administered to 9,918 students.

Despite the evident limitations of the study in terms of sampling and test construction, some of the findings were revealing because they were unexpected. Many results pointed clearly to hypotheses that should be tested in a carefully conducted full-scale survey. The hypotheses involved curriculum and sociological factors. When the variance between countries for a given subject was expressed as a percent of the average within-country variance for all subjects tested it was found that this figure was 6 percent for reading comprehension, 16 percent for mathematics, 5 percent for science, 14 percent for geography, and 12 percent for nonverbal ability. This result was surprising since it was expected by some that the international variance for nonverbal ability would be least.

The more detailed results of this pilot study have already been published.[2] Apart from supplying information that was extremely useful in generating hypotheses for the project of the IEA, the pilot study demonstrated that it was possible and meaningful to carry out an international project of this kind on a fairly large scale.

The Cross-National Study of Mathematics

It was decided in June 1960 to embark on a cross-national study in one subject area, sampling several populations within secondary education by random techniques and using a specially constructed testing instrument. The subject chosen was mathematics. The primary reason for this choice was that most countries involved were concerned with improving their scientific and technical education, at the base of which lies knowledge of mathematics. Second, many recent national and international surveys, such as those carried out by the National Science Foundation in the United States and by the Organization for Economic Cooperation and Development in Europe, have reexamined the curricula and the methods of teaching mathematics and various higher branches of mathematics. Third, the so-called new mathematics had been introduced to varying degrees in some of the participating countries. Fourth, since the symbols of arithmetic and mathematics are largely international, problems of semantics and language would be reduced.

By 1963 research centers in twelve countries had committed themselves to participation in the study.[3] Each participating country bore its own costs for the research, and the United States Office of Education made a grant to cover the international costs.

The effects of several variables upon achievement in mathematics were studied, with the following main results:[4]

1. Variables related to selected school policies

    a. The age of school entry (ages five, six, or seven) appeared to have little differential effect on achievement in mathematics at age thirteen.

    b. Those who completed secondary education between ages eighteen and eighteen and a half showed better achievement in mathematics than those completing between the ages of nineteen and twenty.

c. Smaller classes were associated with superior attainment in mathematics at the higher levels, but this trend was reversed at the lower levels.

d. Reduction in the number of subjects studied was not necessarily accompanied by an increase in achievement in mathematics.

e. Younger students (age thirteen) in schools of 800 pupils or more did better in mathematics than the same age group in smaller schools. Among selective academic schools, those with enrollments between 700 and 1,100 achieved higher scores than any other group, including the larger schools with enrollments over 1,100.

2. Variables related directly to pupil characteristics

a. A low positive relationship was found between achievement in mathematics and attitudes toward mathematics.

b. There was a positive relationship between interest in mathematics and achievement.

c. The between-countries correlations between achievement in mathematics and attitudes toward mathematics were consistently negative and, for the younger populations, surprisingly high. The negative correlations for the younger populations between mean achievement and desire to take more mathematics may have been a result of pressure toward high achievement in mathematics, since the correlations between achievement and the belief that mathematics was important for these populations were positive.

3. Variables related to teacher preparation

a. In general, the more training a teacher had received, the better was his students' achievement in mathematics. Among thirteen-year-olds, the means of the pupils of university-trained teachers were significantly higher than for pupils of teachers trained elsewhere, but this difference was not observed for students at the preuniversity level.

b. Within countries the correlations between the teachers' perceptions of the degree of freedom given to teachers and achievement in mathematics were close to zero, and often negative.

4. Variables related to learning conditions

a. High correlations were found between "opportunity to learn" mathematics and actual achievement. ("Opportunity to learn" was determined by asking teachers to check each test item as to whether it was taught in the school.)

   b. Hours per week spent on mathematics (instruction as well as homework) had only a weak association with achievement in mathematics.

5. Variables related to sex of students

   a. In all countries (except possibly the United States and Israel) more males than females studied mathematics.

   b. In each population boys scored higher than girls on achievement in mathematics, even when other factors were held constant. Except in two countries (France and England) boys had more interest in mathematics than girls.

   c. Where learning conditions were more similar, the differences in achievement in mathematics between boys and girls were markedly reduced. Sex differences in achievement, however, are a within-country phenomenon. In view of the large between-country differences in score it is clear that, although the girls of one country were lower in their mathematics achievement than the boys of that same country, there were a number of countries where the "inferior" girls were superior to the males of other countries.

6. Variables related to social class

   a. A socioeconomic bias existed in all countries in the sense that the preuniversity-year group differed from the thirteen-year-old group in having a higher proportion of students whose fathers had upper- or middle-class occupations. The degree of bias was markedly greater in countries operating a selective system and reached a very high level in some of these countries. It was also closely related to the age at which selection occurred, being greater at the younger ages.

   b. Correlations between rural-urban background and achievement were low. At the preuniversity level only Belgium, the Netherlands, and the United States had significant correlations, and these were positive.

The Cross-National Study of Six Subjects

Beginning in 1966 a much more complex study was undertaken involving achievement in the following areas: science, reading comprehension, literature, civic education, French as a foreign language, and English as a foreign language.[5] In this study three international populations were identified: Population I included all students in full-time schooling aged ten years to ten years, eleven months, at the time of testing; Population II consisted of all students in full-time schooling aged fourteen years to fourteen years, eleven months; and Population IV encompassed all students in the terminal year of full-time secondary education programs that were either preuniversity programs or programs of the same length. The interpretation of this definition of Population IV varied as well as the percent of an age group in the population. There was also a Population III, which was nationally defined for local purposes; results from tests administered to this population were not used in the international analyses. The above definitions held for science, reading comprehension, literature, and civic education. In the case of English and French as foreign languages a further condition was that the students should be currently studying the language and should have studied it for at least two years. Table 1-1 shows the school subjects tested at the various population levels in each of the countries participating in the study.

There was some variation from subject to subject in the kinds of performance outcomes tested. In general, however, both cognitive and affective outcomes were studied. In the field of science, for example, tests were developed to indicate knowledge of various fields (earth science, physics, chemistry, biology); to indicate general understanding of science; to measure practical (laboratory) skills; and to measure ability to use higher-level cognitive skills (application, analysis, and synthesis) in relation to scientific subject matter. On the affective side, there were measures of interest in and attitude toward science. Information was also obtained that permitted some description of the nature of science teaching.

In the field of reading, the tests were to measure reading comprehension, word knowledge, and speed. In the related field of literature, scores were obtained on the comprehension and interpretation of literature as well as on attitudinal responses to it.

Where English or French was taught as a foreign language, information was obtained on reading, listening, writing, and speaking skills as well as on interest in learning the language, on its utility, and on activities out of school that involved use of the language.

Table 1-1
Subject areas and populations tested by country

Country	Science I	Science II	Science IV	Reading comprehension I	Reading comprehension II	Reading comprehension IV	Literature II	Literature IV	French I	French II	French IV	English II	English IV	Civic education I	Civic education II	Civic education IV
Australia		x	x	x	x	x	x	x				x	x			
Belgium (Flemish)	x	x	x	x	x	x	x	x				x	x			
Belgium (French)	x	x	x	x	x	x	x	x				x	x			
Chile	x	x	x	x	x	x	x	x			x		x			
England	x	x	x	x	x	x	x	x		x	x					
Federal Republic of Germany	x	x	x	x	x	x				x		x	x	x	x	x
Finland	x	x	x	x	x	x	x	x				x	x			
France			x										x			
Hungary	x	x	x	x	x	x										
India	x	x	x	x	x	x										
Iran	x	x	x	x	x	x	x	x						x	x	x
Ireland														x	x	x
Israel	x	x	x	x	x	x						x	x	x	x	
Italy	x	x		x	x	x	x	x				x	x	x	x	
Japan	x	x														
Netherlands	x	x	x	x	x	x			x	x	x	x	x	x	x	x
New Zealand		x	x	x		x	x	x	x	x	x					
Poland										x	x					
Rumania										x	x					
Scotland	x	x	x	x	x	x				x	x					x
Sweden	x	x	x	x	x	x	x	x			x	x	x			x
Thailand	x	x	x	x	x	x						x	x			
United States	x	x	x	x	x	x			x	x	x	x	x			x

Source: "What Do Children Know?" ed. T. Neville Postlethwaite, *Comparative Education Review* (entire issue), 18 (June 1974): 162.

In the area of civic education tests were developed to yield a total "cognitive" score as well as subscores on citizenship, institutions, processes, and ability to use simple, complex, and abstract behaviors. There were also tests to measure attitudinal outcomes as well as knowledge about "how the society works."

Three to five years of developmental work were required to construct measures of performance in each subject at each level. The resulting tests produced accurate scores (that is, they were reliable), and national subject panels judged the tests to be appropriate for testing what was to be learned in school (that is, the tests were regarded as valid). Formats of the tests included multiple-choice, open-ended, and fill-in items. For foreign languages tape recorders were used in tests of listening comprehension and speaking.

A series of background questions was also given to the students, teachers, and school principals in questionnaire booklets. The variables on which data were obtained for any one subject at any one level numbered approximately 200 to 500. The amount of information collected (over 150,000,000 pieces) makes this study one of the largest ever to be undertaken in the field of education.[6]

The aims of the research were to identify those factors accounting for differences between countries, between schools, and between students. The technique used was a cross-sectional survey at three different levels. The result, therefore, is a description of education as it is and not as it might be. There are no direct measures of past events. A longitudinal study would have produced such measures, but for various reasons the IEA felt that the time and money required for such a study were beyond its reach. It was necessary, therefore, to use surrogate measures.

The data on input and process variables were collected from students and school personnel by questionnaires. It should be recognized that responses to questionnaires may not be accurate and that they may provide only an incomplete and often indirect indication of the phenomena in which one is interested. These limitations should be borne in mind when one is interpreting the results.

Probability samples of schools and students within schools were drawn for each level for each subject (or group of subjects) within each country. The manner in which the samples were drawn, together with the resulting standard errors of sampling and design effects for selected variables, has been shown elsewhere in detail.[7]

In a paper prepared by the Organization for Economic Cooperation and Development it is suggested that the achievement scores obtained in the IEA study constitute indicators of knowledge and skills transmitted.[8] The IEA, however, has always stressed that it is not conducting a "cognitive Olympics" and that great care should be exercised when one compares the mean scores of various countries. First, although international tests have been constructed, and each country was happy to use them, they were not completely valid for every country. Some countries, for example, may stress objectives that were not measured by the tests. Second, the proportion of an age group attending school varies from country to country, even at the same population level, thus making comparison difficult.

One important factor has not yet been mentioned: this study was conducted in twenty-two nations where altogether fifteen different languages of instruction are used. In spite of problems of translation and the difficulties of planning and executing such a project, not to mention the research skills required by so many people in so many countries, it has been possible to measure outcomes in a reliable way and to make meaningful comparisons. Although there was a certain variation in the quality of the research competencies possessed by the participating centers, the standard form of research proved to be very effective in raising the standards to the highest common factor. It also allowed the educational system of each nation to be seen in an international context.

Selected Findings

With the limited number of observations of country mean scores it is not possible to undertake between-country multivariate analyses, but comparisons of means and distributions can be of some interest. In what follows four different modes of presentation have been used. For reading comprehension the pass-fail rate on particular items is given. For science the increment in general science performance from one population level to another is presented. For literature a profile of four different aspects of literature is given. For the other subjects means and standard deviations are presented.

Reading

Perhaps the most dramatic finding is the very large difference in performance between developed and developing nations. Among developed countries the differences in reading are fairly modest, but the three developing countries fall far below those with a relatively high level of economic development and a long-standing tradition of universal education. The differences exist at both the ten- and fourteen-year-old levels. The point may be illustrated by considering one passage from the battery of reading tests for ten-year-olds:

One of the most interesting birds I have seen is the Indian Tailor Bird. It is a small olive green bird that doesn't look at all unusual, yet it has a most unusual way of making its nest. The birds work together in pairs. First they find a leaf, the right size, and make holes along the edges with their beaks. Through these holes they thread grass. One bird pushes the thread from the outside, while the other bird sits in the nest and pushes it back until the edges of the leaf are sewn together to make a kind of bag, still hanging on the tree, in which the Tailor Bird lays its eggs.

1. What does the Tailor Bird use in place of thread?
   A. Grass
   B. String
   C. Spider web
   D. Thorns
2. The Tailor Birds are interesting because they
   A. are small and olive green in color
   B. live in pairs
   C. make their nests in a special way
   D. fly very fast
3. The Tailor Bird got the name because it
   A. is a small bird
   B. looks unusual
   C. can sew
   D. has a beak shaped like a needle
4. The Tailor Birds make their nests
   A. from leaves
   B. in a hole in a tree
   C. in the tall grass
   D. with a lining of grass
5. The person who wrote about Tailor Birds was trying to
   A. give you some new information
   B. tell you a story
   C. get you to share his feelings
   D. keep you guessing on how the story will come out.

It is clear that the little paragraph shown here is at a level that presents difficulties to a substantial portion of ten-year-olds in every country. (See Table 1-2.) Considering all fourteen countries and all five items, the typical percent failing to get correct answers to all five questions runs between 35 and 40. The median goes as low as 26 percent in Finland, but is 48 percent in Chile, 58 percent in India, and 65 percent in Iran. When one considers that random marking would be expected to give only 75 percent error on these choices of four items, it becomes clear that even this passage is pushing the limit of competence of most ten-year-olds in the three developing countries (Chile, India, and Iran).

Similar results were obtained for Populations II and IV. In one passage for Population II the median error rate was approximately 30 percent, but in Chile, India, and Iran the rate was 47 percent, 66 percent, and 68 percent, respectively.[9] (For further discussion of the results of reading tests, see Chapter 4.)

A further indication of the low level of competence in the developing countries is provided by error rate on the first nine items of the test of reading speed. The following is a sample item:

Peter has a little dog. The dog is black with a white spot on his back and one white leg. The color of Peter's dog is mostly
                        black   brown   grey

In the European countries, a typical error rate on these items is

Table 1-2
Percent failing five items on Tailor Bird passage
Population I (ten-year-olds)

Country	Item 1	Item 2	Item 3	Item 4	Item 5
Belgium (Flemish)	5	44	53	40	43
Belgium (French)	12	27	52	27	30
Chile	16	48	53	41	60
England	10	37	37	27	37
Finland	16	36	26	22	31
Hungary	8	40	32	39	48
India	16	66	58	54	61
Iran	56	75	65	56	66
Israel	12	49	42	46	56
Italy	8	32	80	23	32
Netherlands	8	28	48	41	38
Scotland	11	38	35	30	38
Sweden	10	35	39	27	36
United States	13	35	46	38	33

Source: Robert L. Thorndike, *Reading Comprehension in Fifteen Countries,* International Studies in Evaluation, Vol. III (New York: John Wiley; Stockholm: Almqvist & Wiksell, 1973), 134.

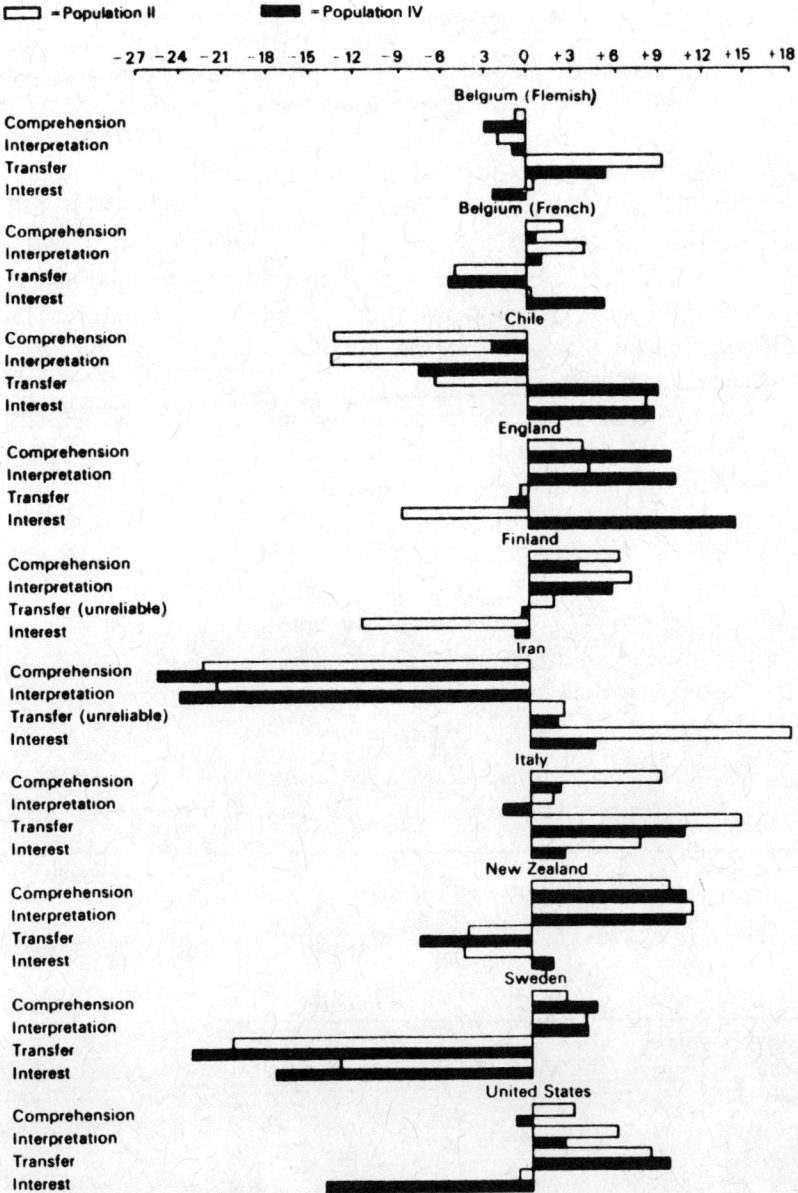

Figure 1-1

Country score profiles on literature tests based on standard scores (All countries mean = 0.) (from Alan C. Purves, *Literature Education in Ten Countries*, International Studies in Evaluation, Vol. II [New York: John Wiley; Stockholm: Almqvist & Wiksell, 1973], 284) about 10 percent for ten-year-olds and 4 percent for fourteen-year-olds. With these values, one must contrast percents of 26, 36, and 52 for ten-year-olds of the developing countries (Chile, India, Iran) and 16 percent, 33 percent, and 20 percent for the fourteen-year-olds. It must be admitted that this material was given as a speed test, but it was also given as a comprehension test. If a substantial proportion of the students in a school system have real difficulty in reading these materials, one must question whether any more than a minimal level of literacy has been achieved in that system.

Literature

Literature was only tested for Populations II and IV in ten countries. Figure 1-1 presents a country profile of four scores; in it "comprehension" is a reading comprehension score of literary prose; "interpretation" is an interpretation (primarily inference) score of literary prose; "transfer" is a measure of the extent to which a student brings his literary experiences to bear on the rest of his life and vice versa; "interest" is a measure of the amount of interest a student expressed in reading literature.

It can be seen that the achievement scores (that is, comprehension

Table 1-3

Means and standard deviations for combined scores
on comprehension and interpretation of literature

Country	Fourteen-year-olds			Terminal secondary students		
	Mean[a]	Standard deviation	Number of students	Mean[a]	Standard deviation	Number of students
Belgium (Flemish)	13.8	6.8	671	20.2	5.7	464
Belgium (French)	15.9	7.0	548	21.5	6.1	1,080
Chile	9.3	7.4	1,058	18.2	6.6	1,681
England	16.1	8.4	3,029	26.4	5.4	2,103
Finland	17.2	7.3	2,242	23.8	5.4	1,583
Iran	6.0	5.0	1,254	8.1	5.3	1,193
Italy	16.4	6.4	7,228	21.0	6.4	14,204
New Zealand	18.7	7.8	1,890	26.8	4.6	1,650
Sweden	15.9	7.8	2,128	23.3	6.4	2,584
United States	16.5	8.8	3,344	21.9	7.7	2,472

[a]Score out of thirty-seven items maximum.

Source: Purves, *Literature Education in Ten Countries*, Appendix V, Table 1, p. 381.

and interpretation) are lower in Chile and Iran than in the participating developed countries. Table 1-3 reports the means, standard deviations, and number of students by country for the combined score of comprehension and interpretation. The results in transfer and interest are presented in Figure 1-1 as an illustration of noncognitive outcomes of an educational system. It should be pointed out, however, that probably the most important measure in literature was the response-preference measure, where each student responded to the measure three times—once in a questionnaire about literary works generally and twice as responses to two literary extracts.

The response-preference measure sought to determine the characteristic way by which a group of students approached a particular literary work or literature in general. For example, some students might be more concerned with the historical aspects of the work, other students with its aesthetic form, others with its theme or meaning, and still others with its affective value. Students in both Populations II and IV were asked to indicate the questions they thought most important with reference to each of two short stories and with reference to literature in general.

A multivariate analysis of variance indicated that students' response preferences were strongly influenced by the nature of the selection that they read, by their age, and by their country. Secondary school students in all countries examined appeared to have learned to focus their critical attention on certain aspects of literary works. A comparison of the preferences of students with those of the teachers of literature shows that the students learned to approximate the response patterns of their teachers.

The study of response preference also indicates clear similarities and differences between countries in the ways students approach literary work. Certain cultural patterns emerge. Students in Chile, England, and New Zealand are similar to each other in their interest in formal aspects of literary works. Students in Belgium, Finland, and the United States exhibit interest in the thematic aspects of the work. Students in Italy are primarily concerned with the historical aspects of the work.

Science

In the report on science the authors have broken down the total score in science into a series of subscores by subject (earth science, physics, chemistry, biology, and practical science) and by type of objective (functional knowledge, comprehension of scientific principles, application of knowledge for problem solving, and analysis, synthesis, and evaluation).[10]

The country-by-country profiles of such subscores help to identify the relative strengths and weaknesses of the performances of the students. Item analyses show not only the percent of the population answering the item correctly (which could be construed as a criterion-referenced test) but also the types of wrong answers typically produced. Both the profiles and the item analyses can be extremely useful to curriculum developers as checks on the extent to which performance matches the global and detailed objectives set for science education in a particular country. The profiles and item anal-' yses can also be especially important where different curricula exist for different school types or regions within a country.

Because there were anchor (common) items in the tests for the various populations it was possible to bring the test scores of the populations onto a common scale and examine the increment from one population level to another in science, as measured by the IEA tests. Figure 1-2 shows such increases. The developing countries are shown separately, and the difference in position of the zero points on the two charts should be noted. The "retentivity" figure given next to the name of the country is an estimate of the percent of an age group still in school in the preuniversity year. It is also at the level of Population IV that the differences in interpretation of the constituency of that population have operated to enhance differences between countries. Children in Australia and New Zealand were not tested at the ten-year-old level, and Japan did not administer the test to Population IV. France administered the science test only to Population IV so that no measure of increment could be obtained. In Figure 1-2 the left-hand side of the white bar represents the scaled mean score at age ten and the right-hand side the scaled mean score at age fourteen; the right-hand side of the solid bar represents the scaled mean score of the preuniversity-year group.

Experience suggests that boys show a greater interest in science than girls and perform better on science tests. These impressions receive powerful support from the IEA study. The differences exist across all countries and increase as the students grow older. Thus, boys performed on the average about one-quarter of a standard deviation better than girls at ten years of age, one-half a standard

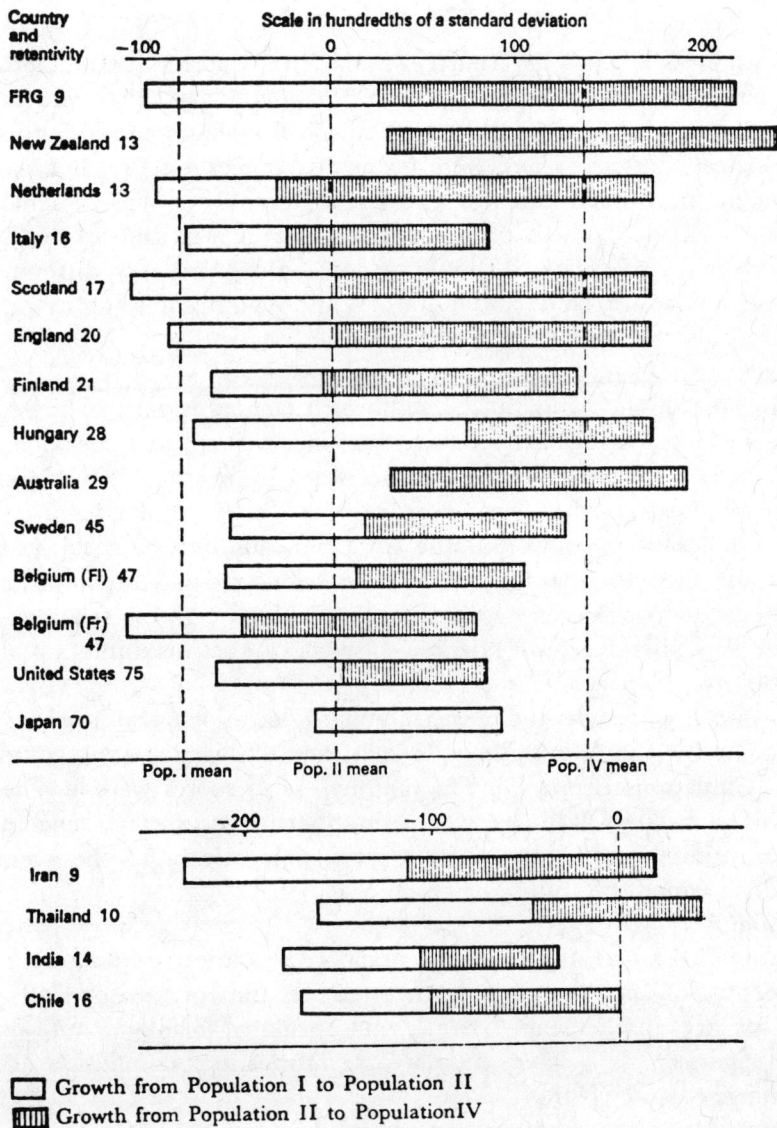

Country
and
retentivity

Scale in hundredths of a standard deviation

-100   0   100   200

FRG 9

New Zealand 13

Netherlands 13

Italy 16

Scotland 17

England 20

Finland 21

Hungary 28

Australia 29

Sweden 45

Belgium (Fl) 47

Belgium (Fr) 47

United States 75

Japan 70

Pop. I mean   Pop. II mean   Pop. IV mean

-200   -100   0

Iran 9

Thailand 10

India 14

Chile 16

☐ Growth from Population I to Population II
▥ Growth from Population II to Population IV

Figure 1-2

Increase in level of performance in science from the ten-year-old level to the terminal secondary school stage (from L. C. Comber and John P. Keeves, *Science Education in Nineteen Countries,* International Studies in Evaluation, Vol. I [New York: John Wiley; Stockholm: Almqvist & Wiksell, 1973], 171) deviation better at age fourteen, and three-quarters of a standard deviation better in the terminal year of secondary education. Boys are more strongly attracted to the physical sciences and girls to the biological sciences. There were fewer differences in scores in biology than in the other branches. The sex differences in science achievement clearly present a problem that deserves attention in the near future in all countries. It should be pointed out that such differences do not occur in reading and literature, although in the latter case girls perform better than boys in half the countries.

French

In both French and English as foreign languages each of the four major skills was tested: reading, listening, writing, and speaking. In the case of listening (where tape recorders were used) and speaking (where tape recorders were used in individually administered tests) subsamples of the main sample were typically drawn. A subsample was also used for the analysis of the test of writing, which was hand scored. For writing and speaking a particular weighting schema was used; it is, therefore, not possible to speak of a set maximum number of points.

Table 1-4 presents the means, standard deviations, and numbers of students for the four skills in French for each participating country for Populations II and IV. The national mean scores were in general highly correlated with the average number of years that French had been studied and average scores related negatively to the average grade in which the study of French began.[11]

English

Table 1-5 presents the means, standard deviations, and number of students for the participating countries in the four major skills of reading, comprehension, writing, and speaking. Blanks denote nonparticipation. The large standard deviations for Population II in reading are noteworthy.

Civic Education

As has been noted, many outcomes of civic education were measured. In Table 1-6 means for total scores on the civics cognitive test are compared for different countries within populations. Comparisons between populations are not possible because the cognitive tests were composed of different items for each population. The phenomenon of considerably lower scores for less developed nations, noted in the other subjects, holds true in civics for Iran.

Table 1-4
Means, standard deviations, and numbers of students for scores in four major skills of French

Population by country	Reading			Listening			Total writing			Speaking fluency		
	Mean	Standard deviation	Number of students	Mean	Standard deviation	Number of students	Mean	Standard deviation	Number of students	Mean	Standard deviation	Number of students
II	(35 items)			(40 items)			(32 items plus composition)					
England	9.3	9.2	2076	9.6	9.7	455	38.4	27.0	437	53.6	32.5	102
Netherlands	12.8	7.8	1545	-	-	-	-	-	-	-	-	-
New Zealand	12.2	8.3	1794	4.5	6.3	1790	45.6	27.3	909	58.8	30.3	185
Rumania	26.8	8.7	2271	24.1	12.5	117	60.1	31.8	1826	97.2	25.4	64
Scotland	13.1	9.8	835	8.8	8.4	834	49.2	31.4	826	64.4	32.5	193
United States	7.6	7.5	4177	6.1	7.2	1927	46.6	27.7	2329	59.2	27.9	174
IV	(39 items)			(40 items)			(32 items plus composition)					
Chile	6.6	5.7	1440	3.2	5.1	173	28.0	21.9	149	28.3	25.1	132
England	32.1	5.2	702	27.9	7.3	180	86.4	28.5	181	111.4	34.1	83
Netherlands	26.3	6.1	1753	-	-	-	-	-	-	-	-	-
New Zealand	27.4	5.4	363	12.8	8.3	361	73.2	26.0	363	93.1	29.3	150
Rumania	28.6	8.7	2247	26.2	11.9	77	62.4	33.0	2073	137.6	39.4	64
Scotland	25.2	7.0	972	17.3	8.9	972	79.3	30.1	966	96.6	32.3	237
Sweden	19.6	9.4	1755	19.3	10.2	1742	67.4	28.2	1670	107.9	41.8	186
United States	17.5	9.5	3069	13.8	11.5	1370	57.6	27.3	1776	91.8	37.1	178

Table 1-5
Means, standard deviations, and numbers of students for scores in four major skills of English

Population by country	Reading			Listening			Total writing			Speaking fluency		
	Mean	Standard deviation	Number of students	Mean	Standard deviation	Number of students	Mean	Standard deviation	Number of students	Mean	Standard deviation	Number of students
II	(60 items)			(24 items)			(31 items plus composition)					
Belgium (French)	22.8	15.2	687	15.4	8.4	671	12.5	6.8	697	20.9	7.4	162
Federal Republic of Germany	29.9	16.2	1074	-	-	-	-	-	-	-	-	-
Finland	16.7	17.8	2100	12.1	9.9	2118	9.7	8.4	2087	19.8	9.7	200
Israel	26.3	18.7	1065	-	-	-	-	-	-	-	-	-
Italy	18.6	17.3	791	9.1	6.0	694	11.3	7.0	731	19.8	7.7	71
Netherlands	37.4	16.4	2090	-	-	-	-	-	-	-	-	-
Thailand	18.4	13.4	1951	-	-	-	-	-	-	-	-	-
IV	(60 items)			(36 items)			(31 items plus composition)					
Belgium (French)	24.2	10.8	1440	16.9	7.0	1394	20.5	6.0	1391	24.2	6.9	192
Chile	10.6	9.8	2118	7.1	4.5	231	7.2	4.8	183	14.4	6.5	94
Federal Republic of Germany	41.3	6.1	1374	-	-	-	-	-	-	-	-	-
Finland	35.6	8.3	2310	23.2	6.1	2296	26.6	3.2	2238	29.9	8.7	279
Hungary	20.1	11.2	1063	16.3	7.3	1063	18.2	7.2	1063	30.3	12.3	119
Israel	27.4	12.9	604	-	-	-	-	-	-	-	-	-
Italy	20.2	12.6	324	14.7	7.6	314	18.9	6.0	322	27.0	7.2	28
Netherlands	42.9	6.5	1561	-	-	-	-	-	-	-	-	-
Sweden	39.5	9.0	1626	26.2	5.4	1602	25.3	4.6	1544	34.0	8.8	197
Thailand	19.7	9.1	937	-	-	-	-	-	-	-	-	-

Table 1-6
Means, standard deviations, and numbers of students
for scores in three outcomes in civic education

Students by country	Total cognitive score			Antiauthoritarian (attitude)		
	Mean	Standard deviation	Number of students	Mean	Standard deviation	Number of students
Ten-year-olds	(41 items)			(10 items)		
Federal Republic of Germany	13.9	8.5	1070	3.4	.6	1051
Israel	-	-	-	3.3	.6	402
Italy	18.6	11.1	2390	3.5	.6	2325
Netherlands	15.6	7.6	1746	3.4	.6	1730
Fourteen-year-olds	(47 items)			(10 items)		
Federal Republic of Germany	26.0	8.7	1313	4.0	.5	1275
Finland	24.5	9.8	2370	3.9	.6	2356
Iran	9.7	5.9	2204	3.2	.5	2032
Ireland	20.8	10.4	834	3.9	.6	817
Israel	25.6	9.6	1039	3.7	.6	952
Italy	22.9	9.4	930	3.9	.6	918
Netherlands	27.3	7.9	1685	4.1	.5	1645
New Zealand	24.3	9.6	1983	4.1	.5	1969
United States	24.7	9.9	3186	4.0	.5	3119
Terminal secondary students	(48 items)			(10 items)		
Federal Republic of Germany	28.2	5.8	1163	4.6	.4	1176
Finland	26.1	6.6	2315	4.3	.4	2282
Iran	6.8	4.9	2159	3.5	.5	2028
Ireland	16.9	8.4	786	4.2	.4	782
Netherlands	25.5	6.5	1296	4.3	.5	1203
New Zealand	28.4	7.1	1665	4.3	.4	1668
Sweden	27.0	7.8	1723	4.5	.5	1636
United States	21.4	9.7	3016	4.1	.5	2928

Mean scores for other countries are clustered fairly closely. It is interesting to note, however, that for Ireland both Population II and Population IV show relatively low mean scores.

The results on the scale of antiauthoritarianism, which is derived from a series of attitudinal items concerning democratic values and which was administered in the same form at each level, can be compared across populations. Antiauthoritarianism is a good characterization of the first major attitudinal factor derived in factor analysis on the fourteen-year-old students and was used as a criterion in the regression analysis that is briefly summarized later in this chapter and completely presented elsewhere.[12] Between-country and between-population differences lead to interesting speculations. Of more interest, however, are patterns of attitudinal difference, which are, unfortunately, too complex to be examined here. One example must suffice: in some countries high antiauthoritarianism is combined with a low sense of being an effective citizen; in other countries both types of attitudes are low.

Additional Findings

With so few degrees of freedom it was not possible to carry out a multivariate analysis between countries to identify the factors associated with differences between national mean scores. Certain differences in some factors, however, are striking and provide interesting leads. Four examples are given below.

Opportunity to Learn

In each school in which science was tested the science teachers in that school were asked collectively to rate each item in the science tests as to the percent of students in the target population who had had the "opportunity to learn" the substance tested in the item, that is to say, the topic had been covered in class. An item was rated "4" if the teacher felt all students had the opportunity to learn what was required to answer the item correctly; "3" if more than 75 percent had the opportunity; "2" if between 25 and 74 percent had the opportunity; "1" if fewer than 25 percent had the opportunity; and "0" if none of the students had the opportunity. Despite its crudity, the measure shows a considerable difference between countries when ratings are summed to a national level. Figure 1—3 presents graphs of "opportunity to learn" against science total test scores for Populations I, II, and IV. Except for ten-year-olds, the relationships are striking.

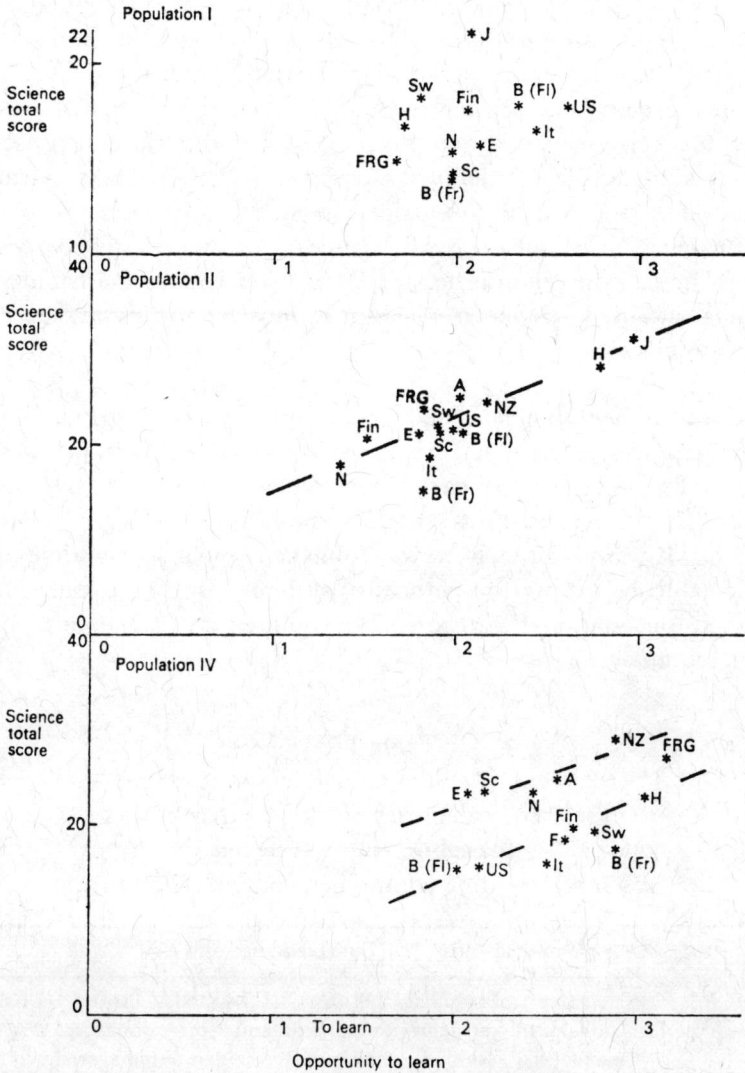

Figure 1-3
Graphs of opportunity to learn against science total test scores for
Populations I, II, and IV (from Comber and Keeves, *Science Education in Nineteen Countries,* 161)

But one cannot help wondering if, for example, in Population II the tests are more appropriate for Japan than for the Netherlands and if students in the Netherlands are learning other things in science not measured by the science tests. That is for the curriculum developers to decide, but it should be pointed out that the test construction was a lengthy and detailed exercise involving science educators in all countries, and all countries agreed that the tests provided a reasonable general measure of science as taught at the particular level. The lack of relationship for Population I may be attributed to the unstructured science curriculum in most countries at that stage of schooling.

Social Bias

There has been much recent discussion concerning the equality of participation of students from all social classes in the whole school system. In the IEA study each research center utilized its own set of social class categories, thus making comparisons between countries difficult. It was possible, however, to make comparisons within countries. Table 1-7 shows the percent of students for each population in selected occupational categories (as defined by the country) for seven countries.

Table 1-7
Percent of students for each population
in selected categories of father's occupation
(based on students tested
in science, reading comprehension, and literature)

Country	Ten-year-olds		Fourteen-year-olds		Terminal secondary students	
	Profes-sional and managerial	Unskilled and semi-skilled	Profes-sional and managerial	Unskilled and semi-skilled	Profes-sional and managerial	Unskilled and semi-skilled
England	16	21	14	14	38	5
Federal Republic of Germany	13	7	14	8	49	1
Finland	9	35	10	34	20	15
Hungary	15	43	20	36	38	18
Netherlands	26	12	20	12	55	5
Sweden	23	31	26	27	35	15
United States	24	18	31	16	34	14

The progression from population to population is of interest, and the difference between England, the Federal Republic of Germany, and the Netherlands on the one hand and Finland, Hungary, Sweden, and United States on the other hand is striking. It should be recalled that the Federal Republic of Germany only tested students in the *Oberprimaria* in the *Gymnasium*.

Enrollment Ratios and Mean Performance

One of the major policy issues in education for the past generation has been whether to move from selective secondary education to comprehensive secondary education. One of the arguments against "going comprehensive" has been that such a step would lower the average achievement of students in the schools of a nation. Analysis of data from the science test suggests that the differences in achievement of the top students are not related to the differences among nations in the percent of an age group enrolled in school. It appears, therefore, that having larger proportions of an age group enrolled is not necessarily accompanied by lower achievement, at least among the top students. These analyses are discussed more fully in Chapter 5 of this volume.

Types of Variables Influencing Achievement

Within countries the student score in the various subjects was used as the school outcome (dependent variable), and the input and process factors were used as the independent variables in a regression analysis where an attempt was made to identify the importance of groups of variables in accounting for variance among students in their performance. Certain groups of variables were formed. The details of how the groups were formed, both through the sieving and compositing of variables, are given in the various reports and particularly in the technical volume by Peaker.[13] For each subject there were, as mentioned above, some 500 independent variables describing the students' home background, their previous and current schooling, the teachers and their teaching, the school principal, the organization of the school, its size and budget, and the like.

The major groups (or blocks) of variables used were as follows:

1. Student characteristics. These variables were home background (a weighted composite of father's education, mother's education, father's occupation, number of books in the home, use of dictionary in the home, and size of family); sex; and age.

2. Type of school and/or program. The elements of each variable

depicting the school or program in which a student was enrolled at the time of testing were criterion scaled against reading, word knowledge, or science to form the variables "type of school" and/or "type of program." These variables were intended as surrogates (perhaps weak ones) for previous schooling.

3. Learning conditions. These included various components of learning conditions. In French and English the amount of prior instruction in the language was treated as a separate block. In the other subjects it was included with other variables reflecting school practices, training of teachers, and other characteristics of teachers.

4. Kindred variables. Among these were expected occupation, attitudes toward education, and the like.[14]

Within countries two major types of analyses were undertaken—between students and between schools. The between-school analysis was undertaken only for science, reading comprehension, and literature. In each case the sieving of independent variables (particularly the instructional, school organization, and kindred variables) was based on partial correlations (after home background and/or type of school or type of program had been partialed out) exceeding twice the standard error of sampling and on the importance attached to particular variables by the subject committee. In this way, the effect of learning conditions could be judged after the caliber of input of students to the school had been taken into account.[15]

Table 1-8 presents a summary showing the total variance explained by the tree blocks "home background," "type of school," and "learning conditions" in the between-student analysis for each subject.

Regression analyses were done on data from Populations I, II, and IV for each country and for each subject to obtain estimates of the total variance accounted for by the three block variables. The results showed that the average percent of total variance accounted for was 38.9, leaving a substantial amount of unaccounted for variance. It was found that the total variance accounted for was notably lower in the developing countries.

Variables related to home background accounted for an average of 11.5 percent of the total variance, with a range from 1 percent to 30 percent. Learning conditions accounted for an average of 10 percent of the variance across all populations in all countries, with a range from 1 percent to 52 percent. On the learning conditions the percents of variance accounted for were clearly lower for reading comprehension, literature, and civic education than for science, French, and English. That is to say, after home background of the students has been taken into account the differences between schools in learning conditions are associated to a considerable degree with differences between students in performance in the subjects under consideration. In some cases, the learning conditions account for two-thirds of the total variance.

One wonders why these differences between learning conditions should be more important for science, French, and English than for reading comprehension, literature, and civics. Is it that the first three are more school oriented in that specialized knowledge is being learned in areas where there is little support received from the home background? Or is it that reading comprehension is not systematically taught in schools once the mechanics of reading have been mastered? Would we expect learning conditions to be more closely associated with student performance if reading comprehension were taught systematically? Is the same true for the learning of the kinds of knowledge in civics and literature tested by the IEA tests?

For the details of the between-school analyses, readers are referred to the main publications of the IEA study, but an example is given here for Population II in Scotland and Sweden, based on data from the science tests. Table 1-9 shows that when the home background of students is aggregated to the school level (the neighborhood effect) the difference between Scotland and Sweden in the percent of variance accounted for is dramatic. In Scotland the society is clearly stratified by home background in its housing and the provision of district schools, whereas the difference between neighborhoods in Sweden is minimal. That is to say, school neighborhoods are more homogeneous in Scotland. With the home background accounting for so much variance in Scotland there is clearly little variance left to be accounted for by other variables such as learning conditions. In contrast, in Sweden, with its relatively homogeneous society, the differences between schools as they are presently run accounts for two-thirds of the total variation. It should be noted that two variables—father's education and mother's education—had to be omitted from the home backgound composite in Sweden because of an ambiguity in the translation of the testing instrument, but it is unlikely that inclusion of these data would have increased the variance accounted for by home background (8 percent) to more than 10 percent.

In those cases where differences exist in the amount of variance

Table 1-8
Average and ranges (in percents) of contributions by selected blocks to total variance in the between-student analyses for each subject (all countries)

Home background (Block 1)

Subject	Ten-year-olds		Fourteen-year-olds		Terminal secondary students	
	Average	Range	Average	Range	Average	Range
Science	11	1-27	16	3-29	13	3-25
Reading comprehension	14	1-25	16	1-27	8	1-18
Literature	-	-	15	5-25	9	4-17
Civics (cog.)	-	-	16	9-20	10	5-18
French (reading)	-	-	15	3-15	4	1-16
English (reading)	-	-	14	1-26	7	1-16

Previous schooling (Block 2)

Subject	Ten-year-olds		Fourteen-year-olds		Terminal secondary students	
	Average	Range	Average	Range	Average	Range
Science	1	0-14	6	0-17	6	0-26
Reading comprehension	1	0- 9	10	0-21	7	0-19
Literature	-	-	8	0-14	3	0- 7
Civics	-	-	11	5-20	5	0-15
French	-	-	22	1-22	3	0- 9
English	-	-	20	0-52	9	0-31

Learning conditions (Block 3 for Science, Reading comprehension, Literature and Civics; Blocks 3 and 4 for French and English)

Subject	Ten-year-olds		Fourteen-year-olds		Terminal secondary students	
	Average	Range	Average	Range	Average	Range
Science	8	1-21	9	4-23	15	4-41
Reading comprehension	6	2-18	6	3-10	5	2-15
Literature	-	-	7	3-12	4	1- 6
Civics	-	-	11	3-18	5	1- 9
French[a]	-	-	17	12-24	19	10-52
English	-	-	16	8-27	17	4-29

Total variance explained[b] (The total variance is always unity or in this case unity x 100.)

Subject	Ten-year-olds		Fourteen-year-olds		Terminal secondary students	
	Average	Range	Average	Range	Average	Range
Science	27	14-36	36	17-55	39	11-63
Reading comprehension	28	18-39	39	20-51	25	13-47
Literature	-	-	55	36-66	37	28-53
Civics	-	-	59	55-62	39	28-57
French[a]	-	-	45	28-65	43	27-61
English	-	-	60	47-79	44	22-75

[a] This is with Reading as the criterion. For Listening the percents accounted for are are greater.

[b] It will be noted that the sum of the percents of the three blocks for any one subject do not total to the percent in the "total variance" block. This is because the "total variance" in each subject is the sum of the first three blocks plus a kindred variables block and typically one or two other blocks which vary from subject to subject but which usually include a Word Knowledge score which might be regarded as a partial surrogate for "intelligence" and "previous experiences" not measured in Blocks 1 and 2.

Table 1-9

Percent of variance accounted for by certain variables
in Sweden and Scotland (Population II, science)

Variable	Scotland	Sweden
Home background	80	8
Age	1	-
Sex	0	5
Type of program	2	28
Learning conditions	3	16
Kindred	2	6
Total	89	63

accounted for by learning conditions, once the home background of students is taken into account, it is useful to identify the factors that appear to constitute influential learning conditions. In general, the following factors stand out as important from the IEA data:

1. Time, that is, the years of study, the number of hours of instruction, and the time spent in homework per week, proved to be important. Unfortunately, however, the IEA study did not examine the trade-off. If, for example, a student who spends more time on science performs better than one who spends less time, how does the latter perform in some other aspect of school behavior on which he has spent more time than the former?

2. The "opportunity to learn" (or, in more general terms, the curriculum) is significant in that the more a student is allowed to learn a subject the more he is likely to learn. This variable is, in general, a powerful one and deserves further study by curriculum planners.

3. The amount of teacher education, including preservice teacher training, is important for the performance of students, particularly in the higher grades in school.

4. The extent to which the students and teacher speak in the foreign language is of consequence in the study of a foreign language. This does not imply, however, that total use of the direct method will produce high standards of performance in all aspects of the foreign language. In the study of French the major variables emerging from the multivariate analyses are consistently time, aptitude, interest, and quality of instruction, in that order of importance.

5. Classroom climate and such practices as patriotic rituals in the classroom were associated strongly with variation in civic attitudes and to a lesser extent with the cognitive scores on the civics test.

Concluding Observations

The worthwhileness of the findings will depend to a great extent on the way in which policymakers, at whatever level, understand both the strengths and weaknesses of the study. This will depend in many cases largely on the systematic links already forged, or in the process of being forged, between the IEA researchers at the national level and policymakers in each nation. The descriptive statistics on so many input, process, and output variables for various levels in each school system are a mine of information for each national system of education. Some of the between-nation differences, as can be seen from the selected examples given earlier in this chapter, have very pointed messages for some national systems. More will surely be provided in a forthcoming report.[16]

The within-country analyses, despite the problems of correlations between the variables in the final regression analysis and exogenous variables have identified aspects of learning conditions (as they now exist) that are highly associated with differences in student achievement and that suggest further experimentation and research.

In a cross-sectional study of this kind, cause and effect cannot be proven, only inferred, and there is a strong case for submitting some of the variables shown to be important to strict experimentation.

IEA is in the process of establishing a data bank of all this information. Certain parts of the IEA data were never analyzed (for example, that concerning students specializing in science at the pre-university level, or concerning budgetary matters); this must be done. Analyses within countries were based on total national samples. It is important to undertake regression analyses on specific subgroups (whether within school type, social class, or minority subgroups) to discover the deviations from the overall findings for such subgroups. Although many variables did not attain "significance" and were therefore eliminated, certain of them are important to different disciplines of education. Their interrelationships with other variables, possible compositing, and differential "effects" on educational output should be explored. Many of the variables that emerged as important can be coded. Will economists undertake cost-effectiveness analyses using these data?

For international organizations one of the problems emerging from the IEA study concerns the types of variables on which it would be useful to collect systematically standardized data.

To return to the first result presented in this chapter, what sorts of pilot work can be undertaken to determine how one can collect reliable data (at low cost) from national samples of children in developing countries where the illiteracy rate is high? What types of interdisciplinary work should be done in developing countries to help identify the types of factors on which data should be collected to help "explain" differences between students and between schools?

Although evaluators do conceptualize in their roles as researchers, it is clear that in all countries the state of the art of educational theory (or in some cases perhaps the communication of it to the educational researchers and evaluators) is poor, as witnessed by the low total variances accounted for. What types of work can be undertaken to improve this state of affairs?

Finally, it is through evaluation projects of this kind that more "hard" information can be collected and used to improve education in the coming years. The knowledge explosion in measurement and evaluation techniques has been rapid. The cooperative nature of the IEA work has helped researchers in some countries to advance their competency by twenty years in a five-year period. More such enterprises of this kind are needed. Research centers and agencies awarding grants should not be deterred by the absence, in many instances, of definitive results. Progress is always slow but decisions concerning the future content and strategies of education must surely be ameliorated by the presence of more research findings.

Notes

1. The twelve countries were Belgium, England, Finland, France, Germany, Israel, Poland, Scotland, Sweden, Switzerland, the United States, and Yugoslavia.

2. *Educational Achievements of Thirteen-Year-Olds in Twelve Countries*, ed. Arthur W. Foshay (Hamburg: UNESCO Institute of Education, 1962).

3. The twelve countries were Australia, Belgium, England, Finland, France, Germany, Israel, Japan, the Netherlands, Scotland, Sweden, and the United States.

4. *International Study of Achievement in Mathematics: A Comparison of Twelve Countries,* Vols. I and II, ed. Torsten Husén (Stockholm: Almqvist & Wiksell, 1967).

5. The results of the study are being published under the following titles: L. C. Comber and John P. Keeves, *Science Education in Nineteen Countries: An Empirical Study,* International Studies in Evaluation, Vol. I (New York: John Wiley; Stockholm: Almqvist & Wiksell, 1973); Alan C. Purves, *Literature Education in Ten Countries: An Empirical Study,* International Studies in Evaluation, Vol. II (New York: John Wiley; Stockholm: Almqvist & Wiksell, 1973); Robert L. Thorndike, *Reading Comprehension Education in Fifteen Countries: An Empirical Study,* International Studies in Evaluation, Vol. III (New York: John Wiley; Stockholm: Almqvist & Wiksell, 1973); E. Glyn Lewis, *English as a Foreign Language in Ten Countries: An Empirical Study,* International Studies in Evaluation, Vol. IV (Stockholm: Almqvist & Wiksell, in press); John B. Carroll, *French as a Foreign Language in Seven Countries: An Empirical Study,* International Studies in Evaluation, Vol. V (Stockholm: Almqvist & Wiksell, in press); Ronald F. Farnen, Sixten Marklund, A. N. Oppenheim, and Judith V. Torney, *Civic Education in Ten Countries: An Empirical Study,* International Studies in Evaluation, Vol. VI (Stockholm: Almqvist & Wiksell, in press); A. H. Passow *et al., The National Case Study: An Empirical Comparative Study of Twenty-One Educational Systems* (Stockholm: Almqvist & Wiksell, in press); G. F. Peaker, *An Empirical Study of Education in Twenty-One Countries: A Technical Report* (Stockholm: Almqvist & Wiksell, in press); David A. Walker, *The IEA Six-Subject Survey: An Empirical Study of Education in Twenty-One Countries* (Stockholm: Almqvist & Wiksell, in press).

6. Information on certain variables was obtained in every country. Each country had, in addition, the opportunity to ask further questions that were of specific interest for its own system. Hence, although this paper presents the findings of the international analyses, each national center will be publishing a national report using a fuller set of data. Three examples of national reports are those of Australia, Japan, and Sweden. See Malcolm J. Rosier, *Science Achievement in Australian Secondary Schools* (Hawthorn, Australia: Australian Council for Educational Research, 1973); Shigeru Shimada *et al., International Survey of Science Education: Report of Japanese National Commission of IEA,* Vol. I (Tokyo: National Institute for Educational Research, 1973); Torsten Husén *et al., Naturorienterande ämnen* (Stockholm: Almqvist & Wiksell, 1973). See also "What Do Children Know?" ed. T. Neville Postlethwaite, *Comparative Education Review* (entire issue) 18 (June 1974): 155-329.

7. Peaker, *op. cit.*

8. Organization for Economic Cooperation and Development, *A Framework for Educational Indicators to Guide Government Decisions* (Paris: Organization for Economic Cooperation and Development, 1973).

9. Thorndike, *op. cit.*, 133-39.

10. *Taxonomy of Educational Objectives: Handbook 1, Cognitive Domain,* ed. Benjamin S. Bloom (New York: David McKay Company, 1956).

11. John B. Carroll, "Factors Accounting for Between-student, Between-school, and Between-nation Differences in Performance in French as a Foreign

Language," paper presented at the annual meeting of the American Educational Research Association, New Orleans, February 1973.

12. Farnen, Marklund, Oppenheim, and Torney, *op. cit.*
13. Peaker, *op. cit.*
14. *Ibid.*
15. Cases of detected high multicolinearity were "solved" by compositing the variables in question. Where the variables related to the school and teacher were based on fewer than fifty observations (that is, fifty schools) there is a problem of stability of estimates. The populations in this category are the two Belgiums (Populations II and IV), Iran (all populations), and the Netherlands and Hungary (Population IV). It should also be pointed out that, where 20 percent or more of the data for a variable was missing, that variable was eliminated from the analysis. This was the case for all data relating to the school budget. Some variables (for example, class size, laboratory class size) were omitted because their relationships with achievement were not linear.
16. Passow *et al.*, *op. cit.*

2. Policy Making and International Studies in Educational Evaluation

William J. Platt

It is my understanding that the IEA, in conceiving and organizing its remarkable studies in educational evaluation, did not try to focus on specific policy issues. Its purposes were, instead, those of basic research: to advance comparative education; and to increase understanding of educational productivity by relating variations in input and process factors with variations in educational outcomes in each of six subjects, between countries, between schools within countries, and between students within countries. It would appear likely that such a broad endeavor would have impact on educational policy. However, the *basic* character of the inquiry's purpose means that most policy implications must be derived, inferred, or deduced from the findings. Policy implications thus are not directly answerable by confirmation or denial of hypotheses guiding a few critical analyses, as might be the case for a study on specific policy issues.

Without at this point trying to judge what potential the IEA studies may have for educational policies, I feel it may be useful to list some specific issues facing educational decision makers. Though cultural traditions and sociopolitical values may be so strong that there is no latitude for decision in certain matters, there are some policy options for school systems serving ten-, fourteen-, and

33

eighteen-year-olds. Some of these options are listed here, although no attempt is made to include concerns dealing with educational objectives:[1]

a. Selective education versus comprehensive education. Sometimes termed "retentivity," this issue concerns the fraction of the age group to be retained in school and the admission criteria at each level. "How many students should be brought how far?"

b. Alternative types of schools and programs to provide streaming of various kinds versus comprehensive schools serving a variety of educational purposes (interschool differentiation); and the criteria for assigning students within these patterns.

c. Homogeneous or heterogeneous ability groupings within schools (intraschool differentiation).

d. Spatial allocations of educational resources, including urban-rural balances.

e. Sex-segregated versus coeducational schooling.

f. Alternative policies regarding repetition versus automatic promotion.

g. Graded versus nongraded organization for instruction.

h. Uninterrupted sequence for attendance for those of school age versus interruptions and multiple reentry.

i. Homework and other requirements for students' efforts outside school hours.

j. Number of students assigned per teacher.

k. Number of students per school.

l. Alternative allocations of hours of instruction among subjects.

m. Alternative ages and other characteristics of students as related to the introduction and continuation of various subjects.

n. Varying emphases placed within the domain of cognitive skills (that is, between knowledge, comprehension, application, analysis, synthesis, evaluation) or between cognitive and noncognitive behaviors such as self-awareness, social skills, and the like.

o. Alternative levels and types of preparation for teachers and other instructional personnel, both preservice and in-service.

p. Alternative compensation schemes for instructional personnel, both in relation to other occupations and as differentiated within the occupation according to experience, performance, evidence of professional development, and so forth.

q. Autocratic versus democratic relations among students, parents, teachers, and administrators.

r. Alternative teaching-learning strategies.

Needless to say, data on only part of the above policy options are to be found in the IEA studies. Such limitations arise from difficulties of measurement and from financial and temporal restraints on the studies. And for some of the options above, empirical experience is not yet available. For example, there is as yet little actual practice of an arrangement by which the lifelong education option of exit and reentry into formal schooling may be exercised.

The IEA placed considerable reliance on a single research approach for its studies of educational productivity: cross-sectional correlation and multiple regression. This method, like any analytical technique, has inherent limitations as to its ability to generate valid and unambiguous conclusions about policy concerns of the type listed above. One limitation emanates from the concept of a "natural experiment."[2] Reality in such natural experiments does not necessarily respect the needs that a particular analytical model imposes for definitive conclusions.

Two serious limitations of natural experiments from the viewpoint of the policy maker are: there is often insufficient variation in the "predictor" variables (with small and uncertain effects, one cannot hope for very pointed policy directions); and there are complex interdependencies among the predictor and exogenous variables, thereby making discriminations difficult to establish and to interpret.

Another handicap inherent in the method used by the IEA is its cross-sectional character, that is, its collection of empirical observations at a single point in time. This is to be contrasted with learning processes that are obviously longitudinal, taking place over time and in some cumulative pattern and pattern of decay that is incompletely understood. The studies of the IEA used various surrogates for time-dependent variables, such as number of years of postsecondary schooling as a measure of teacher preparation, or type of school to which the student was assigned as a measure of past achievement. Further, the design included sampling at ages ten, fourteen, and eighteen (or at the final year of secondary education). By using a procedure that "anchored" items common to the tests for the three age populations, the IEA can make useful comparisons of the increment in achievement from one population to another. But all these procedures, however valuable for certain interpretations, are still not the equivalent of the longitudinal tracking of individuals' learning through time.

These limitations are perhaps sufficient to demonstrate that one should not expect too many immediate answers from the IEA studies. Many of the findings may turn out to be null with respect to plausible policy-related hypotheses. Such findings may, however, be traceable as much to weaknesses referred to above as to a lack of causality between predictor and criterion variables.

Following a short methodological detour, I look innocently at the eight dominant features of those results of the three IEA studies available at this writing which would seem to have direct implications for educational policy. By "innocently" I mean that I do not at this stage question the validity of achievement criteria from the standpoint of policy implications. Instead, I accept these criteria as being adequate cross-national instruments for testing the outcome side of educational productivity, noting Husén's statement that "together with Mathematics, these [six] subjects cover practically all the principal academic subjects in the secondary curriculum apart from the classical languages, which are more part of the European tradition than a feature of modern education in an international context."[3]

In the second section of this chapter I express some concerns about the adequacy of criterion measures in reference to an examination of policy implications. My concerns, even if granted, do not detract from the value of the IEA studies, but perhaps they offer cautions against a too facile adoption of certain policies and their implementation.

With the goal of encouraging further advances in educational productivity from the standpoint of policy, I suggest in the third section some next steps that have been made possible by the studies of the IEA. Finally, in the fourth section, I discuss the degree to which the IEA findings may have illuminated each of the policy options presented in this introduction.

Before proceeding to the above matters I must take a short methodological detour, because I believe the analytical procedures used throughout the several studies by the IEA give a bias which results in overstating effects of home background, or nonschool variables, on variations in student outcomes in relation to those of school-based variables.

At least this bias obtains for the way the IEA labeled four main blocks of variables: Block 1, home and student background; Block 2, type of school or course; Block 3, learning conditions in the school; and Block 4, kindred variables of student habits, motivations, and expectations. The authors of the several volumes all devote considerable space to comparing the "explanatory power" of each of the blocks of variables in accounting for variations in achievement, the most interesting comparison naturally being that of variations in learning conditions in the school, as compared with the effects of variations in home background. Given the analytical procedures actually used, it would have been more accurate to have labeled Block 3 "recent learning conditions," which the authors sometimes did, and Blocks 1 and 2 "earlier learning conditions," which would then mean not only home background but also all the effects on achievement up through the year prior to the test (and possibly the year of the test). Let me explain why I assert that the above bias exists unless some relabeling along the lines I suggest is used.

The problem is a technical one deriving from the fact that the predictor variables are not completely independent of one another (called "collinearity"). Even though other procedures are available to handle the problem of collinearity, the IEA used a sequential method, that of successively introducing blocks of predictor variables in a predetermined order. In this approach only the increment to explained variance is assigned to each new set of variables. The sequence was always the following: home and student background; type of school or course; learning conditions in the school; and "kindred" variables of student habits, motivations, and expectations. The rationale for this sequence is that it corresponds to the chronology of learning impacts on the student.

The IEA commitment to the chronology of learning impacts levies a considerable price, because the procedure is not neutral with respect to the several independent variables being tested in the model. The result of this procedure is that the home background set is assigned both its unique contribution to explained variance and jointly explained variance with all other sets. This procedure has the effect of prejudging that interactions among the predictor sets should all be attributed to factors related to home background.

The problem of sequence is important, as all know who have followed the Coleman Report and its reanalyses by critics as well as by the principal author.[4] In the original Coleman study, as in the IEA studies being discussed, school variables appeared to have relatively little power in accounting for variations in achievement—a result that two sets of critics claimed was inevitable from Coleman's having introduced school variables in the analysis of variance after controlling for variables in the background of students.[5] Coleman's defense is that his was a policy study oriented toward identifying what inequalities of input should be eliminated in order to have the greatest effect in correcting educational inequalities. This policy objective led Coleman and his associates to the deliberate use of the technique of undertaking first to remove the effect of factors over which public policy in the provision of educational resources could have no control, such as family backgrounds. Coleman himself grants that the procedure "gives an underestimate of the absolute effects of school factors, insofar as they are responsible for some of the variance in achievement already explained by family background, but a better estimate of the relative effects than does the standardized regression coefficient."[6]

While Coleman defended his use of sequencing school variables in second place after student background variables on the grounds of the particular policy issue he was trying to illuminate, the same rationale does not apply to the studies of the IEA. These studies were not to focus on a single main policy issue, but instead had the more basic purpose of contributing to an understanding of educational productivity.

IEA could have employed other procedures, including the use of alternative sequences, that is, one sequence having the effect of underestimating the absolute effects of school factors and the other sequence of underestimating the absolute effects of student background factors; or the use of symmetric measures in the way described by Coleman in his reanalysis.[7] In the second approach the question is how much of the predictable variance can be uniquely attributed to each set of the independent variables, and how much is attributable to the joint effects of various combinations of the predictor variables.[8] The authors of the IEA volumes should, at a minimum, have warned readers that, with blocks of interdependent predictor variables, the procedure used (that of sequentially finding additional variance explained) understates the absolute effects of secondary and subsequent blocks of variables, relative to blocks introduced earlier.

Recognizing the commitment of the IEA to simulate the chronology of learning by treating the several blocks of variables as surrogates for time-based influences, I feel that the asymmetrical procedure of the IEA has had the effect of treating Blocks 1 and 2 as "earlier conditions of learning," meaning all those up to the year before the test, and of treating Block 3 as "recent conditions of learning," meaning school conditions during the year of the test. This is because the interaction (collinearity) contributions to explaining variance, that is, those arising from the interdependence of predictor variables, are all attributed to Blocks 1 and 2 by the sequential procedure. Thus the relabeling would seem to be necessary if the asymmetrical procedure is retained.

Landmarks of the IEA Studies

At the present time there appear to be eight landmarks of the studies of the IEA; they will be discussed below.[9]

Large-Scale and Rigorous Multinational Studies

The survey of six subjects by the IEA represents large-scale multinational collaboration in research on educational phenomena in which twenty countries participated. Some 300 experts were involved in constructing test instruments that were administered in 9,700 schools to approximately 258,000 students and 50,000 teachers. Through the good offices of the IEA, the participating countries reached agreement on common sets of achievement measures for testing carefully drawn probability samples of student populations at three age levels. The participating countries now have in their own national centers the test results and data on some 500 inputs and process variables per subject. This data bank alone is of fundamental importance as a contribution to the infrastructure for a variety of future national and transnational inquiries.

The work of the IEA has advanced the state of the art in understanding educational productivity. It has sifted the huge amounts of data collected for many of the possible relationships. Some less rewarding possibilities can now be set aside. The findings offer interesting clues as to ways to improve educational practice, but most of these clues must now be translated into experimentation going beyond the collection of empirical data in natural experiments, as will be discussed further in the next section.

This is an opportunity to acknowledge the vision of the members of the IEA in conceiving the studies and to salute their diplomatic, managerial, and technical abilities in accomplishing such a monumental logistical and organizational task. Credit should also go to the several agencies and institutions that contributed funds to support this project. All those interested in international educational development are the beneficiaries of the accomplishment of the IEA.

Home Background and Age of Students as Predictors of Achievement

The studies found that home background is, in general, the best predictor of achievement and that students in older populations sampled achieve better on the criterion measures than students in younger populations. Even though the effect of variations in home and student background on achievement may be overstated in the studies because of analytical procedures used, these variations are important nonetheless. An implication for policy formation, although unacceptable, is that if the objective of education were simply to maximize achievement scores for a given educational budget, one would be led to an elitist policy of admission to schools all along the line. Such an arrangement would, of course, violate the widely accepted principle of the democratization of education. This principle was reaffirmed by representatives of 130 member governments meeting in the UNESCO General Conference of 1972. Much of the report of the International Commission for the Development of Education deals with aspects of this issue.[10]

The IEA results illuminate the issue of how many people can be brought along how far under alternative strategies of selectivity. The evidence shows that the performance of more able students is not adversely affected when a higher proportion of the age group is retained in the upper grades. Indeed, it would appear the policies of universal attendance do bring more people farther along.[11] Whether the cost of such an achievement is justified is a matter of policy. But the decision of policy makers relates to the values a society attaches to equalizing educational opportunity and to the resources it is willing to commit to attaining this goal.

It is not surprising that older students outperform younger ones. If one accepts the finding of the IEA, however, that school variations other than those presented below show little or no association with variations in achievement, one might conclude that the "growth" in achievement from age ten to fourteen and from age fourteen to eighteen is primarily the result of maturation. In the report of the IEA on achievement in literature, Purves remarks, nonetheless, that growth patterns differ not simply in degree, but also in kind, since students in different countries display different patterns of response. He infers, therefore, that "the differences result from education rather than from a general progress through adolescence."[12] But in the studies of both reading comprehension and literature it is difficult to partial out what part of the growth to attribute to environmental influences outside the school, what part to the school, and what part to the individual's own intrinsic maturation.

I deliberately linked the finding that older populations outperform younger populations with the finding that variations in home backgrounds appear to predict a considerable degree of variation in achievement. I did so because the first tends to suggest that schools make a difference, while the second tends to imply they make little difference relative to home backgrounds. This ambiguity seems to be inherent in the state of our knowledge about education and learning. Since most of the large-scale, cross-sectional studies using correlation and multiple regression techniques also arrived at this same uncertainty,[13] it would appear that there is some kind of principle of uncertainty operating here, which cannot be penetrated by existing analytical techniques, and that new and more powerful research approaches are needed.

Achievements in Science

Variations in achievement in science are associated with the opportunity a student has to study science in school, with the time he gives to studying it, with the curricular emphasis a school system places on science education, and with his teachers' total postsecondary education. In addition, boys achieve higher than girls in science, and the gap widens with age.

Extra interest could well attend the IEA science inquiry for several reasons. Learning in science seems more likely to be school based than the other subjects treated. Further, other large-scale inquiries had been made into factors associated with verbal and reading achievement, where nonschool effects can, a priori, be substantial, as indeed they proved to be in the Coleman and Jencks studies. It can be said, in general, that the IEA results show that *some* aspects of schooling (but relatively few of the many hypothesized) do make a difference in science achievement. And, if one accepts my criticism that the IEA analytical procedure overstates the effects of home background, the few effects that schools appear to have on science achievements are robust indeed. It is also to be noted that more of the variation in science achievement can be explained by school-based predictors as the students grow older. This would follow from a consideration that in most of the participating countries there exist opportunities for elementary learning in science in the nonschool environment, whereas more specialized abilities in science become increasingly school based. It may also suggest that the null finding of school effects in reading comprehension may be traceable to the lack of systematic teaching of reading for comprehension comparable to more systematic teaching for science comprehension.

How do the findings with respect to science education relate to policy? When one looks at the input and process variables found to be significant—the opportunity to learn, the student's time in hours per week and cumulative years, the curricular emphasis, the additional years of postsecondary preparation of teachers—one must conclude that excellence in a particular subject like science requires a national and a societal commitment. There is, in short, no easy route to achievement in science; instead, hard work by students, good preparation of teachers, and an educational-cultural commitment are needed. The consistently high performance of science students in Japan (unfortunately not measured at the eighteen-year-old level) suggests that educational values in that society combine to stretch students in science and that the stretching yields results.

One might ask if there are opportunity costs associated with according a high priority to one subject field. Though the analysis does not appear to be able to answer such a question with any precision, the reasonably good correlations in achievement in the three subjects tend to show that the opportunity cost is negligible.

That boys achieve more than girls in science and that the gap widens with age is not surprising, given the expectations accorded the sexes in most participating countries with respect to careers in science. (It should be said that in reading comprehension and in literature, girls slightly outperformed boys in a majority of countries.) What policy implications flow from the results in science?

Unless one accepts the dubious premise of inherent genetic differences between the sexes in aptitude for science, one can only conclude that policies primarily beyond the school ought to work at correcting injustices in career opportunities and in societal discrimination. Failure to do so is unjust; it also results in an economic and social loss to society through underachievement of women. Someone might advance the proposition that society's loss in science is offset by a correspondingly higher achievement in roles a given culture may be willing to assign to its females. But with growing liberation, these possibilities for alternative roles (which are seldom realized in educational provisions) diminish. Further, such an argument, like that referred to above on opportunity cost, presumes that education is a zero-sum game. That it is not is clear from research on learning processes and the unused potentials of the human brain.[14]

One should be able to derive some interesting policy implications from the IEA findings that there exist regularities of common clusters of science achievement within the following four groups of countries: Commonwealth countries; other Northern European countries and the United States; Romance-language countries; and developing countries.[15] This suggests some interaction of educational traditions with student performance, which, if more fully understood, might lead to higher educational productivity.

Literature and Culture

Students' responses to literature, particularly their questioning of it, are related to culture, of which the school is at least a partial agent of transmission and regeneration.

Volume II of the IEA series devotes its longest chapter (eighty-two pages) to analyzing patterns of response to literature, using as an instrument a battery of twenty questions about each literary passage in the test, from which the student was to select five value-relevant questions.[16] The investigators and those who had developed this type of instrument believe the results may illuminate students' critical thinking, the relation of the students' critical thinking to that of teachers, and the interaction of culture upon the students' critical thinking.

The designers of the test instrument for literature had assumed that there would be marked cultural patterns of preference response, and the findings of the study supported this assumption. The study also shows that the national patterns of response tend to polarize somewhat for the older age group tested, although students who achieved high scores did not necessarily conform to this polarization. Further, the findings show that the polarization of students' preference responses tends to move toward their teachers' preference response patterns. The author of the IEA volume infers that schooling has an effect upon responses in literature.

A possible policy implication is that whether or not an explicit effort is made to do so, a given culture, through its school system, does condition its students' responses in reflecting moral, ethical, and judgmental values. To some, this may suggest that those phenomena deserve study as a means of deliberately adjusting curriculum materials and their use to be more nearly congruent with "desirable" patterns, desirable being defined by some sort of cultural or national consensus. To others, this finding may suggest the desirability of a noninterventionist stance, leaving those matters to the unseen hand of the intellectual marketplace.

Performance in Reading Comprehension

Performance in reading comprehension is a better predictor of performance in science or in literature than is achievement in science or in literature a predictor of achievement in the other of the two subjects. This finding merely identifies the expected "central role of reading as a determiner of achievement in the more specific subject matter skills."[17] The policy implication is that priority should be given to this enabling skill.

School-Connected Variables

With few exceptions, including those noted above, most school-connected policy variables (streaming, organization of schools as selective or comprehensive, size of class or school, characteristics of teachers, methods of instruction) show relatively little partial correlation with variations in achievement.

The weakness of most school-based variables in explaining variations in achievement, while a null finding, provides important implications for policy. But before discussing these implications, certain caveats deserve mention. I have suggested that the analytical procedures used have the effect of understating school influences. Further, as I will discuss in the next section, some caution in

e developing countries scored significantly below their counter-
rts in technologically advanced countries. The IEA results present
clear indications of those policies that might help to narrow the
fferentials in achievement. Later in the chapter I present some
utions in accepting the IEA achievement differentials between
veloping and developed countries. At this point I only mention the
equality of resources devoted to education between developing
untries and the rest of the world: the developing countries, with
ree-fourths of the world's children, spend only 8.6 percent of the
rld's education budget.

Regularities in Achievement Comparisons

Interesting implications may be drawn from a further dis-
gregation of test results according to categories of behavioral skills:
nctional information; comprehension; application; and higher
ocesses. In the science study,[18] country profiles are drawn by
ich one can relate test results in these four categories to "oppor-
ity to learn." Opportunity to learn represented the teachers'
imates of the degree to which the school offered opportunities to
quire the four categories of behavioral skills. The similarities
tween national profiles of opportunity to learn and test scores are
iking. They need to be further compared with some of the
tional differences found in the detailed test results in literature, for
ample, where students of certain countries show greater interest in
aluative questions over moral concerns or over aesthetics (or alter-
tive patterns). These patterns should be of considerable interest to
tional officials concerned with educational policy, to those respon-
le for curriculum development, and, of course, to students of
mparative education. For the first time, there now exist some
ss-national calibrations to illuminate such inquiries.

The concept of internationally uniform tests of cognitive skills
ses some problems with which the IEA no doubt struggled. The
cussion that the IEA included in its three initial volumes does not,
wever, allay my concerns, which I shall summarize here.

In the first place, any universal test must use common denomi-
or test items which may fail to measure the precise skills a teacher
even a school system has sought to impart. This problem is
mpounded when a test must be administered across many cultures
presumably many educational objectives. Thus the suitability of

implementing such null findings of the IEA studies sho
served if my reservations about the appropriateness of t
ment criteria are accepted.

The null findings with respect to streaming, size of scho
like, suggest that unit cost comparisons in these matt
become very interesting to policy makers, since cognitiv
are apparently unaffected by these policy variables. In s
of the resources for which some systems have been willin
premium, such as reduced class size, may not be of n
Thus, under the unremitting financial pressures felt in
budgeting everywhere, one would appear to be free, at l
basis of cognitive achievement considerations, to adop
expensive solutions. Why not, for example, let students
(class size) grow, perhaps by several multiples? Since teach
represent a sizable fraction of the budget of all school sy
one action alone could greatly improve the effectiveness-t
of a school system.

It is here that we may be victims of the mismatch b
"natural experiment" examined in the participating coun
one hand, and the resolving power of the analytical proce
on the other. It will be recalled that earlier in the cha
attention to the lack of adequate variation frequently exp
predictor variables. This null finding may, therefore, not
reflect reality, but only the lack of observations over
range of sizes of class.

The IEA findings in science may have implications fo
jects to which policy makers may wish to devote attent
tunity to learn, time invested, curriculum emphasis,
preparation. In other subjects, where school effects
association with variations in achievement, it may be tha
educational production function is operating below a t
minimal effectiveness. If a "threshold phenomenon" a
more powerful educational technologies might well yield
differentiations in outcomes. At least the findings of the
suggest that this hypothesis is worth exploring.

Differences in Levels of Achievement

Large differences in levels of achievement exist betwe
of developing and developed countries; in all three stud

implementing such null findings of the IEA studies should be observed if my reservations about the appropriateness of the achievement criteria are accepted.

The null findings with respect to streaming, size of school, and the
like, suggest that unit cost comparisons in these matters should
become very interesting to policy makers, since cognitive outcomes
are apparently unaffected by these policy variables. In short, many
of the resources for which some systems have been willing to pay a
premium, such as reduced class size, may not be of much value.
Thus, under the unremitting financial pressures felt in educational
budgeting everywhere, one would appear to be free, at least on the
basis of cognitive achievement considerations, to adopt the least
expensive solutions. Why not, for example, let students per teacher
(class size) grow, perhaps by several multiples? Since teachers' salaries
represent a sizable fraction of the budget of all school systems, this
one action alone could greatly improve the effectiveness-to-cost ratio
of a school system.

It is here that we may be victims of the mismatch between the
"natural experiment" examined in the participating countries, on the
one hand, and the resolving power of the analytical procedures used,
on the other. It will be recalled that earlier in the chapter I drew
attention to the lack of adequate variation frequently experienced in
predictor variables. This null finding may, therefore, not necessarily
reflect reality, but only the lack of observations over a sufficient
range of sizes of class.

The IEA findings in science may have implications for other subjects to which policy makers may wish to devote attention: opportunity to learn, time invested, curriculum emphasis, and teacher
preparation. In other subjects, where school effects show little
association with variations in achievement, it may be that the whole
educational production function is operating below a threshold of
minimal effectiveness. If a "threshold phenomenon" applies, then
more powerful educational technologies might well yield meaningful
differentiations in outcomes. At least the findings of the IEA study
suggest that this hypothesis is worth exploring.

Differences in Levels of Achievement

Large differences in levels of achievement exist between students
of developing and developed countries; in all three studies those in

the developing countries scored significantly below their counter-
parts in technologically advanced countries. The IEA results present
no clear indications of those policies that might help to narrow the
differentials in achievement. Later in the chapter I present some
cautions in accepting the IEA achievement differentials between
developing and developed countries. At this point I only mention the
inequality of resources devoted to education between developing
countries and the rest of the world: the developing countries, with
three-fourths of the world's children, spend only 8.6 percent of the
world's education budget.

Regularities in Achievement Comparisons

Interesting implications may be drawn from a further dis-
aggregation of test results according to categories of behavioral skills:
functional information; comprehension; application; and higher
processes. In the science study,[18] country profiles are drawn by
which one can relate test results in these four categories to "opportunity to learn." Opportunity to learn represented the teachers'
estimates of the degree to which the school offered opportunities to
acquire the four categories of behavioral skills. The similarities
between national profiles of opportunity to learn and test scores are
striking. They need to be further compared with some of the
national differences found in the detailed test results in literature, for
example, where students of certain countries show greater interest in
evaluative questions over moral concerns or over aesthetics (or alternative patterns). These patterns should be of considerable interest to
national officials concerned with educational policy, to those responsible for curriculum development, and, of course, to students of
comparative education. For the first time, there now exist some
cross-national calibrations to illuminate such inquiries.

The concept of internationally uniform tests of cognitive skills
poses some problems with which the IEA no doubt struggled. The
discussion that the IEA included in its three initial volumes does not,
however, allay my concerns, which I shall summarize here.

In the first place, any universal test must use common denomi-
nator test items which may fail to measure the precise skills a teacher
or even a school system has sought to impart. This problem is
compounded when a test must be administered across many cultures
and presumably many educational objectives. Thus the suitability of

a test for any particular system or student within a system is a compromise. For some students the congruity of the test with what they have learned and their reasoning styles may be so poor that the students show low achievement even though their true abilities in that subject are considerable.

The voluntary character and high professional standards of the IEA effort were potentially adequate safeguards for this difficulty. Countries cooperated only if they felt the tests, in whose design they had had an opportunity to participate, were sufficiently fair to be useful locally. Yet in Volume III it was admitted that the pretest experience showed that the tasks proposed would be "too difficult" in the developing countries; nonetheless the items were retained. And the results confirmed the pretest experience: "the most dramatic feature of the between-country results is the very large difference between the developed countries . . . and the developing countries."[19]

The editorial and developmental work on the tests was carried out in English, with subsequent translation into the language of the participating country. The abilities to be tested were those common to the participating countries, in which the educational orientation of North America and Western Europe was dominant (except for Japan's participation in science education). Only those items and passages "universally considered acceptable" were included, which may have meant omission of items or content of a non-Western orientation. The format of the tests was primarily multiple choice, a pattern with which Western students are more familiar than are students in other parts of the world.

Jensen speaks to this issue:

It should not be forgotten that intelligence tests as we know them evolved in close conjunction with the educational curricula and instructional methods of Europe and North America. Schooling was not simply invented in a single stroke. It has a long evolutionary history and still heavily bears the imprint of its origins in predominantly aristocratic and upper-class European society. Not only did the content of education help to shape this society, but, even more, the nature of the society shaped the content of education and the methods of instruction for imparting it. If the educational needs and goals of this upper segment of society had been different, and if their modal pattern of abilities— both innate abilities and those acquired in these peculiar environmental circumstances—were different, it seems a safe conjecture that the evaluation of educational content and practices and consequently the character of public education in modern times would be quite different from what it is. And our intelligence tests—assuming we have them under these different conditions—would most likely also have taken on a different character.[20]

The concept of international standardized tests may be running counter to a trend toward individualized instruction and diversity. Much of the advanced practice observed by the International Commission for the Development of Education[21] has as its premise the tailoring of educational offerings to individual needs and learning styles. This premise guides diagnosis of student needs and the pacing of learning challenges. Is it feasible and desirable in view of these trends to apply one universal instrument?

National development itself, whether it be approached from the standpoint of economic, social, cultural, or educational factors, is guided increasingly by an appreciation for, and enhancement of, diversity and pluralism. This is reflected, for example, in the greater emphasis that the objectives for the United Nations Second Development Decade place on the realization of national identity. It is also revealed in the healthy debate on the ethics of development.[22] These trends also suggest the need in educational measurement for diversity more than for uniformity.

My second set of concerns regarding most of the achievement measures used by the IEA involves their preoccupation, with some exceptions, with only part of the cognitive domain and their consequent weaknesses in higher cognitive behaviors of choice, creative insight, divergent thinking, synthesis, and evaluation; and noncognitive behaviors of self-concept and self-awareness and tolerance for other people and for ambiguity and artistic and aesthetic abilities. It should be said that some of the items in the science study do test for the higher cognitive behaviors of analysis, synthesis, and evaluation and that some of the items in the literature test move toward higher cognitive skills. The volume on civic education is not available at this writing, but I understand that it includes some measurements in noncognitive behaviors. But the IEA effort is, on the whole, oriented toward measurement of cognitive, rational behavior. It must be admitted that other behavior traits may go beyond agreed objectives of secondary education in the three subjects whose reports are now available. It must also be admitted that tests for higher cognitive and noncognitive behaviors are not yet well developed, are expensive to administer, and are difficult to interpret.

In the preface to each volume Husén notes that the six subjects, with mathematics, cover practically all the academic subjects of the secondary curriculum. Such coverage invites one to take the composite of the tests and to infer from the skills being tested in them something about the kind of "universal men and women" implicitly under development in the participating countries. The next step in the speculation is to compare the profile of such universal men with other estimates of the skills that may be required for the realization of man's destiny in the twentieth and twenty-first centuries. These other estimates may not be easy to come by, but one can make inferences, for example, from *Learning to Be*.[23]

This comparison is not, of course, fair to the IEA. Faure's men did not have to be described according to the discipline of behaviors and attitudes that could be measured, whereas the IEA authors had to confine themselves to what could be tested in the seven subjects. But the important thing, it seems to me, is to see whether the proficiencies that the IEA is examining are an interesting sample. (I do not require that it be a significant sample.) If it is not, then one should go slowly.

What if education is responsible, as I suggest elsewhere, for assisting individuals to escape from dependency?[24] What if the new skills that should be learned in the educational system before age eighteen are the eight proposed by Coleman—intellectual skills, skills of some occupation, decision-making skills, general physical and mechanical skills, bureaucratic and organizational skills, skills in the care of dependent persons, emergency skills, and verbal communications skills in argumentation and debate?[25] The IEA tests include measures primarily in only the first of these eight skills. Is that coverage sufficient?

Perhaps in the information-rich environment of technologically advanced countries, schools should turn over some responsibilities for teaching certain cognitive skills to other learning resources. The IEA findings seem to show that this is, in fact, already happening. But, on the other hand, schools may have other neglected educative roles that could be within their competence, such as helping students acquire and practice higher cognitive behaviors like abstract reasoning and divergent thinking, as well as proficiencies in the noncognitive domain of self-awareness, teamwork, concern for quality of life, and tolerance.

It will perhaps be argued that IEA could not pursue normative concerns; instead it had to confine its inquiries into what is, rather than what ought to be. This may, realistically, be all that was feasible for the required multinational cooperation. If so, however, the limitations inherent in the criterion measures used must be recognized in drawing on the IEA results for policy formation and implementation.

Policy Formation and Implementation

The question to be addressed in this section is: in the light of the availability of the IEA studies, what next steps of potential benefit to policy formation and implementation can be put forward? I have four suggestions. All of them, to be implemented, would require a healthy partnership between researchers and officials having operational responsibilities.

First is the need for more systematic joint review in regional and international meetings of educational authorities on the implications of the IEA findings for curriculum development, teacher education, and resource allocation. The IEA, as a nongovernmental organization, has been able to move flexibly in getting these landmark studies made. Now it is up to national authorities individually and in their collective action through regional and international organizations to reflect on the findings, to extend them, and to embark on the large-scale experimentation that these studies and other trends in education are encouraging.

There now exist in the participating countries valuable data banks of systematic information on samples of student populations and on input and process variables. Additional countries should be encouraged and, if necessary, aided in acquiring this kind of infrastructure for educational research and evaluation. But the main value, other than that of scholarship, comes when the data bank is linked with educational decision making. Where there are national centers, linkages may already exist. But such linkages do not usually emerge spontaneously; instead they require cultivation and dialogue between researchers and decision makers. For example, whenever a researcher is initiating a new inquiry he should consult appropriate policy makers whose choices might be illuminated by the results of the research.

A way of making the data bank much more useful in examining

policy options would be to add the dimension of cost to as many of the input and process variables as possible. At present the IEA material lends itself mainly to examining the education production function, but, without the dimension of cost, does not lend itself to answering questions about allocation of resources.

Research is particularly needed to develop instruments for measuring educational outcomes in ways appropriate to the needs of non-Western societies and developing countries. As discussed above, the IEA results suggest that the achievement tests used did not represent a satisfactory fit for students in those developing countries which participated. There is good reason to suspect that the tests inadvertently were not culturally fair, that they were overdependent upon reading ability, upon Western concepts and values, and upon experience with the multiple-choice format. The IEA studies also showed that many of the relationships between predictor variables and educational outcome variations in technologically advanced countries were not similarly operative in developing countries. There is, clearly, an opportunity for some basic inquiries into these phenomena, work that will require cross-cultural teams of educators, educational measurement specialists, anthropologists, sociologists, and economists.

For reasons advanced earlier, it is important to extend international measurement of achievement into higher cognitive behaviors (divergent thinking, creativity) and into noncognitive behaviors. The latter measures may need to be quite culture or nation specific, dealing as they do with the affective domain and with aesthetic and political values. It will be interesting to discover how well correlated performance in these behaviors in different cultures is with performance in the simpler cognitive behaviors.

An area that needs to be explored in international educational evaluation is that of teaching-learning styles and strategies, which should include alternative patterns of teacher-student interactions and also alternative learning interactions among students. While variations in school processes thus far have explained little about variations in outcomes, it is still possible that alternative teaching-learning strategies will be influential, particularly with respect to higher cognitive and noncognitive behaviors. In selecting alternative teaching-learning strategies, economic factors should be carefully considered so as to provide a range of unit cost options.

I have argued elsewhere that large-scale experimentation is needed, with educational innovations "vectored" toward lifelong education in society and toward equality of opportunity.[26] The IEA findings can offer hypotheses for guiding the design of such experiments. Where, for example, it has been found that school variables are apparently unrelated to variations in educational outcome, there should be an exploration of the relationship between the effect of a radical variation of the input or process variable and reductions in cost. Similarly where, as in the science studies, factors such as the teacher's education and opportunity to learn have shown positive associations with outcomes, other experiments should be designed to discover empirically the elasticities of these relationships.

In the design of experiments a number of principles should be observed. First, of course, longitudinal measurement, the lack of which is the greatest weakness of cross-sectional analysis, can be used. This entails baseline measurements before experimentation as well as measurement during and after experiments. Second, designs should try to allow for some kind of control, but true comparability between experimental and control groups can seldom be assured in social science research. Third, there ought to be adequate provision for feedback to allow for experiential learning from the experiment. Fourth, the potential for propagation and diffusion of successful experiments should be considered throughout the design and implementation. In short, as Philip Coombs puts it, "there should be a contingency plan for success."

Whoever proposes experimentation (or "planned variation") in education must have answers to legitimate ethical concerns about manipulation and coercion. Following are at least three partial answers:

First, any kind of educational effort is already an intervention by a public or private authority. As such it implies certain value orientations and socialization and academic objectives. For much of traditional educational practice these are not explicit, but are nonetheless operative. And many implicit values are elitist, authoritarian, and inequitable. Any experimentation should, of course, bear the burden of proof that its orientations offer prospects of improvement over the orientations implicit in present practice.

Second, with respect to the concern that experiments may be imposed on unwilling students, parents, schools, or regions, one can always look for those ever-present indigenous innovations that are to be found somewhere in nearly every setting, those promising some progress in dealing with some aspect of educational pathology. By relating and shaping such indigenous innovations to the best available learning theories and the best guides for allocation of resources, we can make progress in experimentation without coercion.

Third, the potential of the Hawthorne Effect should not be neglected in educational experimentation. The Hawthorne Effect is, in simplified terms, the tendency of the participants in an experiment to perform well just because their self-esteem is enhanced through the attention they are receiving. There is no reason why we should not take advantage of this bonus.

If there were general agreement on the need for widespread systematic experimentation in education, then educational authorities would make certain that every project or program that departs significantly from existing educational practice would include a component of systematic experimentation and evaluation. The IEA studies have advanced the state of the art for such evaluation.

The foregoing suggestions and the extension of the IEA work in educational evaluation would benefit greatly by accelerating certain patterns of international cooperation. International networks of information exchanges will greatly facilitate the universal search for means of advancing educational productivity. Such information services, which would report currently on important experiments being undertaken and on the results being obtained, would contribute to the search. A group of agencies interested in international cooperation for educational development is helping the UNESCO International Bureau of Education in Geneva to provide such an educational reporting service. This service could help to put educators and policy makers in touch with each other. The exchanges should concern such technical and organizational matters as ways of developing a research infrastructure, arrangements for linking such an infrastructure to educational decision making, the further development of instruments of evaluation and their adaptation and application to a variety of local conditions, and a clearinghouse service on experimentation that offers the possibility of solving some of the stubborn problems of education.

IEA Studies and Policy Making

In Table 2-1 I return to the several policy options described in the first section of this chapter, indicating how the IEA studies relate to each of the policy concerns listed there. In the table I make the following distinctions: The first column under "IEA findings or data available" is "International inferences," where the findings are reasonably conclusive and universal in relating achievement variations to choices in the options listed. The second column is "Mixed results." Here some conclusive findings relating to achievement variations apply in some countries; often the indicated policy directions are not the same for different countries. "Further analysis indicated," the third column, indicates that interesting data are probably available in the national data banks established as a result of the IEA studies, but further guidance for policy awaits teasing out relationships not yet tested in the IEA volumes. In the fourth column, "Insufficient variation," the predictor variables had insufficient range to allow policy-related interpretations. The fifth column, "Not evaluated," shows that data were not collected that would illuminate this option.

In the following paragraphs I shall summarize policy implications of the IEA studies in reference to the policy options described more fully in the first section of the chapter. (I have not commented on those options not evaluated in the IEA studies, although further research on them may be desirable.)

a. *Retentivity.* The comprehensive or nonselective policy of retaining a larger fraction of the age group increases the yield of an educational system, "yield" being defined as the proportions of a total age group reaching various levels of achievement. It appears, further, that high retentivity brings with it few or no penalties in the performance of high achievers. The IEA studies did not gather information on the cost implications of taking various positions on this policy option. Such positions depend on the value a society places on equality of educational opportunity and on the resources it can commit to achieve this value.

b. *Interschool differentiation.* The absence of significant achievement variation with alternatives in school organization suggests that the policy maker is free to adopt a position on this option according to other criteria, such as minimization of cost or equality of opportunity. It would seem likely that noncognitive outcomes such as

Table 2-1

Relevance of IEA findings to some options in educational policy making

Policy option	IEA findings or data available				
	International inferences	Mixed results	Further analysis indicated	Insufficient variation	Not evaluated
a . Retentivity	x		x		
b . Interschool differentiation	x		x		
c . Intraschool differentiation			x		
d . Spatial allocation of resources					x
e . Sex-segregation versus coeducational schooling		x	x		
f . Repetition versus automatic promotion					
g . Graded-nongraded				x	x
h . Multiple reentry					x
i . Homework		x			
j . Students per teacher	x				
k . Students per school	x				
l . Allocation of instructional hours among subjects	x				
m . Ages for learning various subjects				x	
n . Emphases on behavioral types of skills learned			x		
o . Teacher training		x	x		
p . Teacher compensation			x		x
q . Autocratic versus democratic instruction and administration					x
r . Teaching-learning strategies			x		x

social skills and tolerance for others would, however, be influenced by whether the school organization is comprehensive or differentiated. Noncognitive measures are not included in the three IEA studies at hand, but will be available in the study on civic education.

c. *Intraschool differentiation*. While the raw data on the students' socioeconomic backgrounds collected in the IEA studies would seem to have interesting potential for examining alternative ability groupings and peer group effects, the three summary volumes did not explore these phenomena. It is possible that further analysis would reveal associations between various patterns of intraschool differentiation and variations in achievement. The composition of learning groups by ethnic background, or by socioeconomic characteristics, is at least partially manipulable by policy choices.

e. *Sex-segregation versus coeducation*. The IEA findings are inconclusive as to the effects on achievement of sex-segregated schools. Further analysis of the data collected may be justified.

i. *Homework*. There is some indication that a policy favoring student effort in homework promotes achievement in science. In the other two subjects, on the other hand, the effects of this policy produce only mixed results in the IEA studies. Perhaps this is because these practices are more nearly a reflection of the climate of the school and community or because homework distributions are bimodal: low achievers are required to do extra homework, and high achievers do so voluntarily.

In the IEA results, the variables "parental interest" and "parental help" showed little or mixed effects upon variations in achievement. It is conceivable that policies could be designed to have some influence on such home-connected variables if they had turned out to be important in educational productivity. It is curious, on the other hand, that other home-connected factors such as the family's socioeconomic position and the father's occupation do have important effects, and yet there is little way for educational policy making to influence these variables.

j. *Students per teachers*, and

k. *Students per school*. There is not as much variation in class size as one would like in order to draw strong conclusions. Further, correlations may be hidden by other conditions such as the fact that small classes and small schools are often located in rural areas. Within these limitations, the IEA studies suggest that policy with respect to both unit class size and unit school size can be guided by criteria other than cognitive achievement.

l. *Allocation of instructional hours among subjects.* The results in the science study suggest that achievement is influenced favorably by a serious commitment to the subject as evidenced by adequate allocation of instructional hours and years of study to that subject. Further analysis of test results of all three studies by curriculum specialists would appear to be fruitful. Such analysis could provide both national and multinational feedback to guide the development of particular curriculum materials that should be mastered by students at the several age levels.

n. *Emphases on behavioral types of skills learned.* As discussed in the second section, further analysis and comparative studies would seem to be called for in exploring the implications of the IEA data that disaggregates achievement into its behavioral components. Even if the further analysis reveals regularities between predictor and criterion measures, there will still remain the difficult pedagogical issue of how instruction, in its content and method, can reflect with fidelity any chosen emphases.

o. *Teacher training.* Only in science was there a fairly universal association between teachers' number of years of postsecondary education and achievement. In the other IEA studies the null finding would suggest the policy makers have latitude to use other criteria in determining the proper preparation of teachers. The measures of teacher preparation adopted by the IEA were not discriminating, however, as to the quality of that preparation, which may be the principal reason for the inconclusive findings with respect to achievement.

r. *Teaching-learning strategies.* Data were collected in the IEA studies on a considerable number of teaching practices such as frequency of using small-group work in instruction, tutoring, and so forth. These variables produced only inconclusive effects in attempts to relate them to variations in achievement. It is possible that organizing these data into larger strategies of teaching and learning would yield some useful insights, perhaps if only in respect to certain types of students or to achievement in certain behavioral types of skills.

The international community of educators and policy makers interested in educational development now has a better base of knowledge on which to make some policy decisions than it had before the IEA studies were available. It also has at hand in the national centers of participating countries a data bank that should be linked as a working tool with policy making. Promising paths for additional research have been clarified by the IEA's findings, particularly along lines of systematic experiments in which one can assess the effects on outcomes of more radical, planned variations in inputs and process factors than occur in natural experiments. These experiments should be designed not only to explore possibilities opened up by the IEA results but also to be vectored toward the full realization of human potentials, as is discussed in the report of the International Commission for the Development of Education.[27]

Notes

1. For a current international assessment of educational objectives, see Edgar Faure *et al.*, *Learning to Be* (Paris: UNESCO-Harrap, 1972). Some commentary on redirections in education is included in William J. Platt, "The Faure Report—A Turning Point in Educational Planning," paper presented at the conference on "Science and Man in the Americas," Mexico City, June 1973.

2. Husén says in the foreword to the volume on science: "We . . . conceived of the world as one big educational laboratory where a great variety of practices in terms of school structure and curricula were tried out. We simply wanted to take advantage of the international variability with regard both to the outcomes of the educational systems and the factors which caused differences in those outcomes." L. C. Comber and John Keeves, *Science Education in Nineteen Countries: An Empirical Study*, International Studies in Evaluation, Vol. I (New York: John Wiley; Stockholm: Almqvist & Wiksell, 1973), 10.

3. *Ibid.*, 9.

4. James S. Coleman *et al.*, *Equality of Educational Opportunity* (Washington, D.C.: Government Printing Office, 1966); Frederick Mosteller and Daniel P. Moynihan, *On Equality of Educational Opportunity* (New York: Random House, 1972).

5. Samuel Bowles and Henry M. Levin, "The Determinants of Scholastic Achievement—An Appraisal of Some Recent Evidence," *Journal of Human Resources* 3 (Winter 1968): 3-24.

6. Mosteller and Moynihan, *op. cit.*, 154-56.

7. *Ibid.*, 158-63.

8. Comber and Keeves, *op. cit.*, offers results expressed in unique and joint variance, but only within Blocks 2 and 3, namely those of type of school and learning conditions within the school.

9. *Ibid.*; Alan C. Purves, *Literature Education in Ten Countries: An Empirical Study*, International Studies in Evaluation, Vol. II (New York: John Wiley; Stockholm: Almqvist & Wiksell, 1973); Robert L. Thorndike, *Reading Compre-*

hension Education in Fifteen Countries: An Empirical Study, International Studies in Evaluation, Vol. III (New York: John Wiley; Stockholm: Almqvist & Wiksell, 1973).

10. Faure *et al.*, *op. cit.*
11. This finding confirms the earlier special study of retentivity, which was based on a study of achievement in mathematics in twelve countries. See T. Neville Postlethwaite, *School Organization and Student Achievement* (Stockholm: Almqvist & Wiksell, 1967).
12. Purves, *op. cit.*
13. Henry A. Averch *et al.*, *How Effective Is Schooling? A Critical Reading and Synthesis of Research Findings* (Santa Monica, Calif.: Rand Corporation, 1972). See also Marshall Smith's commentary in the present volume, following Chapter 4.
14. See Faure *et al.*, *op. cit.*, Chapter 5.
15. Comber and Keeves, *op. cit.*, 176.
16. Purves, *op. cit.*, 199-281.
17. Thorndike, *op. cit.*, 175.
18. Comber and Keeves, *op. cit.*, 136-38.
19. Thorndike, *op. cit.* 148.
20. Averch *et al.*, *op. cit.*, 46.
21. Faure *et al.*, *op. cit.*
22. Dennis Goulet, *The Cruel Choice: A New Concept in the Theory of Development* (New York: McClelland and Stewart, 1971).
23. Faure *et al.*, *op. cit.*
24. Platt, *op. cit.*
25. James S. Coleman, "How Do the Young Become Adults?" *Phi Delta Kappan* 54 (December 1972): 226-30.
26. Platt, *op. cit.*
27. Faure *et al.*, *op. cit.*

Commentary

Richard J. Light

The mid-1960s brought what seemed to be the biggest educational survey ever, the Equal Educational Opportunity Survey, carried out so adeptly by James Coleman and his associates. Now the mid-1970s brings an even larger enterprise: the results of the IEA survey. What

This commentary is Dr. Light's summary of the various methodological issues raised during the conference, both in small-group discussions and plenary sessions.

do these surveys tell us about how to improve educational effectiveness? What, in particular, are strengths and weaknesses of using large-scale sample surveys as tools for informing policy? What alternative procedures are available? This question of policy development was a major concern of the Workshop on Data Analysis, as well as other parts of the IEA conference.

Surveys such as those conducted by the IEA inform us about the state of student achievement. They tell us about variation in achievement both within and among many countries. They enable us to estimate for each country the proportion of variation in achievement explained by variations in school resources. But each of these estimates is a descriptive statistic, a description of how things are. Further, while knowledge concerning the proportion of variation in achievement owing to variation in school resources gives an idea of the "importance" of various school resources, it does not suggest the probable effect of changes in the resource mix. Thus, drawing policy inferences from these kinds of survey data becomes difficult.

Consider a hypothetical example. The Minister of Education of a certain country learns that twelve-year-olds in Country A are achieving at much higher levels in all subjects than children of the same age in Country B. He further determines from IEA data that the proportion of variance in achievement explained by variation in school resources (SR) is:

$$R^2_{SR} = 0.05 \text{ in Country A and } R^2_{SR} = 0.20 \text{ in Country B.}$$

What should he do? Do such comparisons help him to make decisions about improving his country's educational system? They do not. In particular, it is not clear how different "relevant importances of variations in school resources" among different countries should be compared. The value of R^2_{SR} depends upon many factors that differ enormously among the countries participating in the IEA. For example, R^2_{SR} for any country depends upon the amount of variation in resources among its existing schools in that country, as well as the amount of variation in family or "home" variables. It also depends upon "selection," how students are chosen to participate in certain subjects. Countries that restrict admission, say, to certain high school subjects based upon prior outstanding achievement in those subjects will, simply because of this selection process, have higher means and lower variances in achievement. It is therefore difficult for one country to draw strong inferences about what might happen if it adopted certain features of another country's educational policies or methods.

The statistical analysis of IEA data raises several issues that blend with policy concerns. Perhaps the broadest question is, when a large body of data on many variables is collected, and when these data are analyzed using several functional forms (the IEA analyses of school effects used multiple linear regression), how does an investigator choose which functional form best describes the data? It is tempting simply to fit different forms to the data (for example, linear, curvilinear, logarithmic, or multiequation models) and choose the form with the highest overall variance (R^2). Yet this is unattractive on two grounds. First, in the extreme case this strategy is no more than curve-fitting. Given enough functional forms as competitors, there is substantial risk of finding a "chance" good fit. Second, and perhaps more important, it is often forgotten that searching for maximum variance sometimes results in an invalid criterion for identifying functional forms.[1]

Other statistical issues raised by the IEA data are narrower, but quite important. Two examples follow. First, how should cross-product terms be entered into regression analyses? No such terms, defined as multiplicative functions of independent variables, were used by the IEA, yet they might identify substantial interaction effects among demographic, family, and school resource variables. Second, how should a group of related variables be aggregated into a single one? The IEA combined many home-based variables in each country into a single "block." This involved weighting each component, with weights assigned judgmentally rather than empirically. This is an important issue for statisticians because different sets of weights could influence findings about the relative importance of variables related to the home.

A final issue here concerns the distinction between micro- and macropolicy inferences. The work of the IEA focuses on national and international analyses and comparisons; discussion thus tends to center on so-called macropolicy issues. But how should these data influence individual policy decisions? Let us take an example. Suppose an analysis shows that in Country A expected earnings for students completing twelve grades are essentially no different from expected earnings for those completing only eleven. In Country B, on the other hand, expected earnings for completing the additional year of schooling are substantial. Is the policy implication that a guidance counselor acting rationally should advise the student in Country A not to bother completing the extra year, while in Country B he should advise the reverse? The answer to this question is complex, depending partially upon personal values and also to some degree upon probabilities of receiving certain rewards. For example, a country can have no increase in expected earnings for the additional year of schooling and nevertheless offer incentives for more schooling. An illustration would be to offer a student a one-in-ten chance at receiving a highly fulfilling or high-prestige job upon graduation that he would have had much less than a one-in-ten chance of getting without the extra schooling. Without traveling far down the branches of the tree of possibilities, we can say that while large-scale surveys in education have focused carefully on macropolicy issues, surprisingly little attention has been paid to how individuals could make rational use of findings from such surveys.

The foregoing sounds negative. Is it impossible to estimate the probable effects of changing certain features of a country's educational system? The answer is no; it is quite possible to estimate the effects of change. The way to do this is to change something. George Box said it well years ago: "To find out what happens to a system when you interfere with it you have to interfere with it."

It was not the charge of the IEA investigators to move into a system and change it. What they did they did well. The primary value of the survey is their development of a comprehensive set of descriptive statistics indicating the state both of school practices and student achievement in many countries. These findings will be useful for years to come. But if a country wishes to learn about an innovation, such as what the impact of a new way of teaching mathematics might be, the country must install this innovation and study it.

The best method for studying the effectiveness of innovations is the randomized controlled field trial. "Field trial" implies that the innovations are being studied in the field rather than in the laboratory. "Controlled" indicates that the choice of innovation for a school or an individual is made by the investigator rather than a "natural" process. "Randomized" refers to the use of chance at some stage to choose which people are exposed to which innovation.

Such trials give us the best inferences about what impact changes or innovations will have. Yet until now few randomized controlled trials have been done in education. This has led many to question if they can be successfully implemented. Yet there are several examples of successful implementation. In the United States, the evaluation of the Emergency School Assistance Program that offered money to school systems to facilitate desegregation was given enormous strength because school systems wishing to receive money were randomly divided into groups that did or did not get some. Evaluations of the new educational television programs "Sesame Street" and "The Electric Company" were designed as randomized trials, and while some difficulties arose in maintaining the integrity of the groups of children and the treatment, again the results were strengthened by the features of control and randomization. Careful planning is usually necessary for such studies. This may require extra time and effort. Yet the benefit of imbedding even a very small randomized controlled field study in a large, continuing innovation is great. Such studies offer the opportunity constantly to improve and update an ongoing program or structural change as new information about its effectiveness becomes available.

In conclusion, what primary themes arise from the IEA analyses? There are at least two with implications for the future.

The first theme involves procedures for collecting data and studying schools. When studying the effectiveness of schools, investigators must ask whether the primary goal is to provide descriptive data of how things are or, rather, to estimate what outcomes would most likely occur if certain changes were introduced. If the goal is essentially description, then large-scale sample surveys provide excellent data. The work of the IEA falls into this category. If, on the other hand, the purpose is to develop informed predictions about how educational outcomes would change in response to new or different mixes of resources, a randomized controlled field trial is preferable, almost necessary.

The second theme involves procedures for analyzing data. Whether the data come from a survey or a controlled field trial, the inferences that emerge depend a great deal upon what relationships an investigator initially postulates. In the past, the linear additive model has been used almost exclusively to connect input variables of school quality and family background with the outcome variable of school achievement. This leads to standard multiple linear regression as a means of analysis, which has the clear advantage of being well known, widely used, and more tractable than most competitors. In the future, it would be desirable to introduce other models as serious competitors to the maximum extent possible. One example is the full logarithmic model frequently used by economists. Drawing policy inferences is rarely an easy business. Being able to choose among a wider array of mathematical forms, each representing a different sort of educational process, might enrich substantially our understanding of policy options.

Note

1. For example, when the true form is logarithmic but we do not have ratio scale measurements on the independent variables (note that most social class measures as well as school attributes follow at best interval scales; they are rarely ratio scales), the presence of arbitrary, additive constants of measurement can produce a case where a linear additive equation, such as that used in the IEA analyses, demonstrates a higher variance (R^2) than the correct logarithmic form. The reverse, on the other hand, cannot happen.

3. Implications of the IEA Studies for Curriculum and Instruction

Benjamin S. Bloom

The International Association for the Evaluation of Educational Achievement (IEA) is an organization of twenty-two national research centers which are engaged in the study of education.[1] It represents a cooperative approach to international research on educational problems. In each country there is a national research center which is involved as a cooperative partner in the cross-national research. This group of research centers has been concerned with the use of international tests, questionnaires, and other methods to relate student achievement and attitudes to instructional, social, and economic factors in each nation. The overall aim of this research is to establish generalizations which will be of value in education, not only in the participating countries, but throughout the world.

In addition to the international reports, each of the national centers is preparing a report in which its nation's results are discussed against the background of the international data and findings. In these national reports each center will highlight the results of its own country's research, explain these results, and suggest their curricular, instructional, and other implications.[2]

Reprinted with permission from *School Review* 82 (May 1974): 413-35. The article was adapted from a paper presented at the IEA conference held at Harvard, November 1973. Minor revisions have been made in the published article.

In this chapter I will attempt to draw some of the overall implications for curriculum and instruction from the major results of the IEA surveys. But the important work on this subject will be the attempt by each of the national research centers to draw implications and suggest hypotheses that will make the greatest sense in terms of its own country's special conditions and problems.

International Instruments and Data Collection

A major feature of the IEA is that its evaluation instruments and data-collection procedures have been developed especially for the purpose of international comparison and study. In previous cross-national studies test items and styles of test construction tended to be specific to the country in which the instruments were constructed. The evaluation instruments developed in one country typically showed that country to be superior to the other countries included in the study.

International Evaluation Instruments

This concern with internationally validated evaluation instruments impelled the IEA to create international as well as national committees in each subject. Both types of committees studied national curricula and examinations and attempted to identify subject-matter content and educational objectives of major significance in the different countries which participated.

The national committees criticized the specifications proposed by the international committee. In addition, they constructed test items and questionnaire procedures, criticized particular proposals of items, did pilot studies on particular features of the instruments, translated the material into the national languages, and conducted national tryouts of the items and procedures.

The international committees finally produced the major evaluation instruments, supervised the procedures for major cross-national studies in each subject field, and took major responsibility for the international report on the results.

Each of the IEA subject studies has taken about seven years to complete, with at least half of this time devoted to instrument construction, criticism, and revision. Every effort has been made to develop valid international instruments based on what the representatives of the countries regard as the most important subject content and educational objectives of the subject field. Nevertheless these instruments are more "fair" to some national curricula and syllabi than to others.

The emphasis on international evaluation/instruments has resulted in the involvement of a large number of persons in each of the participating countries on the national committees, both as critics of the tests and questionnaires and as consultants at different stages in the development of the instrument. This way of working has resulted in a set of evaluation instruments which represent the variety of objectives and content included in the subject field for most of the participating nations. The IEA evaluation instruments give an excellent picture of the state of evaluation and education (objectives and content) in the countries represented in these studies. The evaluation instruments also represent an international consensus on the knowledge and objectives most worth learning.

Evaluation and Education

The IEA has stimulated the development of more adequate evaluation procedures in a high proportion of the countries involved in these studies. There are increased interest in modern evaluation methods, more concern about the subject-matter content and objectives of education, and greater sophistication in using and interpreting evaluation data. In each country, most teachers whose students were tested in the IEA study were asked to review each item in the tests and to judge it in terms of the student's opportunity to learn that idea or process. This procedure has introduced many teachers throughout the world to modern evaluation methods.

As a result of these studies there is a more realistic understanding of what education is accomplishing at present in each country, as well as an awareness of what is being accomplished in other countries and some grasp of the reasons for the international differences. There is also increased concern for the improvment of education and the schools in most of the IEA countries, including interest in more effective curricula and the training of teachers for these new curricula. While I do not wish to claim that the IEA is the major force in encouraging new curriculum work, the IEA methods and instruments, the interaction of educators and evaluators, and the results of the IEA studies are powerful incentives for the development of more adequate curricula and improved teaching-learning approaches within and between IEA countries.

The IEA surveys provide baseline data for each country against which future changes in education may be appraised. The IEA instruments and the increased sophistication about evaluation in each of the countries provide methods and procedures for the systematic evaluation of the effectiveness of new approaches to education. They also make it possible to study alternative approaches on a small scale before major decisions are made to implement the most effective approaches on a larger scale.

Differences between Countries

Perhaps the most dramatic findings of all the IEA studies during the past decade and a half have to do with differences between countries. For highly developed countries there is a difference of about one standard deviation between the means of the highest scoring and lowest scoring of these countries. But there are approximately two standard deviations between the means of the highest of the developed nations and the average of the developing nations.

One can translate these statistics in a number of ways.

If the mean of the highest scoring nation is used as the criterion of what it is possible for students to learn, about 85 percent of the students in the lowest scoring of the developed nations would be below this mean while about 98 percent of the students in the developing nations would be below this point.

If school marks were assigned in the various nations on the basis of the highest nation's standards (where perhaps the lowest fifth might be regarded as failing), then almost 50 percent of the students in the lowest scoring of the developed nations would fail, but about 85 percent of the students in the average developing nation would fail.

These results may also be considered in terms of grade norms. If judged by test results in the highest-scoring nation, the average student in the lowest scoring of the developed nations would be at about the eighth-grade norm after twelve years of schooling, while the average student in the developing nations would be at about the sixth-grade norm after twelve years of schooling. This would be true even when selectivity at the secondary level is held constant. Although one may have misgivings about such attempts to put schooling in terms of age or grade norms in the highest-scoring nation, it is evident that the attainment obtained in one year of schooling in the highest nation requires one and one-half or two years of schooling in less favored nations. To put it in terms of time and human resources spent, it may cost twice as much for a particular level of learning in one place as it does in another.

The IEA studies may be viewed as demonstrating what education can accomplish under the most favorable conditions we can find throughout the world. In principle, any country which so desires may do for its youth what the most favored national system does do for its students. Since there must be many trade-offs, each national system which attempts to do better for its youth must search for ways of accomplishing this—even though it may not necessarily attempt to duplicate the particular pattern of conditions in the other countries.

Opportunity to Learn

Perhaps the most important variable in accounting for the differences between national systems—even where they are equally selective—is the opportunity to learn as judged by teachers. Teachers were asked to evaluate each item in the IEA test as to the proportion of their students who had an opportunity to learn the idea or process underlying that item. When the results for particular groups of teachers and students across a nation are correlated, the IEA studies show a very high relation between these teachers' judgments and the overall performances of the students.

This variable—opportunity to learn—is essentially a description of the curriculum in the local schools and classrooms, perhaps a more direct measure of this curriculum than are the published versions of the official curriculum at the national or local level. The IEA tests were based on the official curriculum in the different nations, and this variable suggests what portion of the official curriculum has survived at the classroom level. Perhaps the most important curriculum implication is that beautiful curriculum plans have little relevance for education unless they are translated into what happens in the classrooms of the nation or community. Until curriculum plans and material affect the classroom they are little more than dead documents to be stored in libraries. If the curriculum is to be brought to life in the classroom, many of the nations will have to provide more preservice and in-service education for teachers. And such training programs will be effective only if they succeed in changing teachers' behaviors in the classroom. Some national curriculum centers have been experimenting with various approaches to these problems, and some of the approaches to in-service education of teachers have been effective. The nations may learn much from each other if they develop a cooperative approach to the study of such teacher-training problems.

Teacher Competence

There is evidence that the competence of teachers in both subject matter and methods of teaching varies greatly between nations. In one developing country a sample of science teachers took the IEA science test and scored below the average secondary school student on the international norms. It is unlikely that students can learn much from teachers who do not thoroughly understand the subject they are teaching. Where the capabilities of the teaching staff are low, a nation which wishes to upgrade its students' learning must either attract more competent teachers, provide more adequate in-service education, or use mass media to supplement what the classroom teacher offers.

If Beeby is correct about the levels of teaching that can be provided by teachers with different levels of postsecondary education,[3] some developing countries must either wait decades before they can provide adequately trained teachers at all levels of schooling or they must find a way in which a small number of well-trained teachers can provide the bulk of instruction through the use of mass media in the classroom. There has been some excellent research on different ways of using radio and television for instructional purposes. Under favorable conditions a small number of very competent teachers can provide high-quality instruction for thousands of students through the use of such media.

Time

A third variable that appears to be important, a combination of curriculum and instruction, is time. Time has been studied in the IEA research in terms of number of years of instruction in a subject, the number of hours of instruction per week or year, and the number of hours of homework per week in a particular subject. Throughout the IEA studies there is a significant relationship between the amount of time the student devotes to a subject and learning in that subject.

Although there is little direct evidence in the IEA research, there is a strong likelihood based on other research that involvement, the percentage of time in class that the student is actively working on a subject, is also a significant element in learning. On the basis of simple observational studies it appears that in some countries students are actively engaged in learning for 90 percent or more of class time, while in other countries students are actively engaged in learning only about 50 percent of the time. Further studies in depth are needed to check these observations. While the amount of time students are actively engaged in learning should be highly related to achievement in the IEA tests, the explanations for differences in degrees of involvement in school learning are more complex and probably include cultural differences, the importance of school learning to students and their parents, ways in which teachers use time available for teaching, the quality of instruction, and the extent to which students are helped to attain the prerequisites for particular learning tasks.

There are no simple suggestions for curriculum and instructional changes which will quickly and drastically alter the picture of national differences reported in the IEA studies. Each nation must decide whether it wishes to do anything about the results reported. If a nation decides to make changes, it is likely that in the short run changing some of the instructional strategies used in the classroom will be most effective. There may be need for changes in curriculum and instruction as well, but it should be recognized that these are costly long-term problems. Perhaps most will be gained in the near future if countries seeking change can find ways of exchanging experience, materials, and personnel so that they may study basic ideas and approaches which have been found to be effective in other nations.

Verbal Education

The IEA studies typically consist of separate samples of students participating in each subject study. But a selected sample of students did participate simultaneously in the studies of literature, science, and reading. The median intercorrelations for these subjects in fifteen countries are shown in Table 3-1.

Table 3-1
Median intercorrelations for literature, science, and reading

Subjects	Students		
	Age 10	Age 14	Final year secondary education
Science versus reading comprehension	.68	.60	.44
Literature versus reading comprehension	-	.68	.54
Science versus literature	-	.41	.28
Science versus literature (holding reading comprehension constant)	-	.00	.05

Several generalizations can be drawn from these correlations.

1. Learning in both science and literature is highly related to reading comprehension. This is true to such a degree that there is almost no residual relation between science and literature when the level of reading comprehension is held constant.

2. Reading comprehension is more highly related to literature than to science.

3. The relation between reading comprehension and science or literature declines with age or grade of school, probably because the schools drop the students less able in reading comprehension.

While the relation between subject-matter competence and word knowledge is somewhat lower, the same generalizations tend to hold. These generalizations are true, almost without exception in each of the nations included in this portion of the IEA studies.

If we view reading comprehension and word knowledge as two facets of what British psychologists term "verbal education," it is apparent that this type of learning tends to dominate and in large part determine what students learn in the schools in all the countries included in the IEA studies.

These two aspects of verbal learning are important because most teacher instruction and most of the learning materials in the schools are verbal. Unless the student can understand the teacher's explanations and instructions, he has difficulty in learning. Verbal skills enable students to learn from the instructional materials even when the teaching is less than adequate.

We might wish that instruction and instructional materials placed less emphasis on reading comprehension and work knowledge, but it will be a long time before this will occur to any significant degree in the schools as they are now organized. Learning in the schools is, now and for the foreseeable future, likely to be based on verbal instruction to groups of students using textbooks and other instructional materials which are largely verbal in nature, with judgements about the student largely based on evaluation procedures using questions and responses that are verbal in form. The early development of verbal ability (vocabulary and reading comprehension) appears to be necessary if the child is to learn well—or even to survive—in school.

Over the past decade studies in the United States, England, Israel, and other countries show that much verbal ability is developed in the home. In the IEA study of reading comprehension the three most important variables related to students' level of reading comprehension are reading resources in the home, socioeconomic status (father's occupation and parents' education), and parents' interest in the child's education and the encouragement they give the child to read.[4] Especially in the ten-year and fourteen-year populations, the home background accounts for more of the student variation than do the school characteristics. This is not true of the eighteen-year population—largely because of the selectivity of the schools at the older ages. (In the United States, where over 75 percent of the students are still in school at eighteen years of age, the home background is still the most important variable in accounting for reading comprehension.)

Throughout the world there appears to be a curriculum and instruction in the home as well as a curriculum and instruction in the school. The effects of the home curriculum and instruction for reading comprehension and word knowledge appear to be so powerful that schools are not able to compensate adequately for the differences already present when children enter school. Differences in verbal ability developed at home before age six are exaggerated by the schools in the period between ages six and ten and the school period between ages ten and fourteen. By age eighteen all students except the most able in verbal ability are weeded out by the schools' selective policies.

Societies which wish to improve children's school learning have only two realistic policies to follow: increase the effectiveness of the early education of children and/or increase the effectiveness of verbal education in the schools, especially during the ages of six to ten.

Early Childhood Education

Many countries are exploring the possibility of providing early childhood education (ages three to six) for children—especially for children who are likely to be deprived because of inadequacies in the home curriculum and instruction. Mass media appear to be quite effective for some kinds of instruction at this age level.

Research in the United States indicates that it is possible to find ways of helping parents to improve some of the learning conditions in the home.[5] When this is done, the results in verbal learning, attitude toward school, and ability to learn in school are likely to be as good as or better than the results obtained through the use of nursery schools alone. Even better results are obtained when parents and nursery schools collaborate in the effort to help the children. Schools may relate to parents in a variety of ways to increase the effectiveness of both the home curriculum and the nursery school curriculum and to strengthen the relations between these curricula in this period of great verbal development of the child.

The Primary School

Both the Coleman Report in the United States[6] and the Plowden Report in England[7] indicate that there is also great language development in the age period six to ten but that there is an increasing amount of individual differences in verbal abilities during these years. That is, whatever differences there are between children at age six in verbal ability are considerably increased during the primary period of schooling. In the various attempts to provide "compensatory" education in the United States and elsewhere, a number of special curricula have been developed which apparently enable the lower third or half of the children to close much of the gap between them and their more favored peers. These curricula emphasize specific instruction in the particular features of language, thought, and reading on which these children appear to be most deficient. Many of these curricula require special techniques of patterned practice in the classroom, a great deal of success on the part of the children supplemented by frequent and varied rewards and reinforcements, and appropriate classroom evaluation and corrective procedures to ensure mastery of each part of the learning process.

Some of the newer procedures stress a closer relation between the primary school and the home so that they mutually support each other. R. H. Dave and Richard Wolf[8] have identified some of the home environmental processes which may be improved when home and school collaborate in improving the child's learning as well as his attitude toward school and school learning.

While there is no point in the child's educational development at which it is too late to improve conditions, there is considerable evidence that the critical point for verbal education in schools as they are presently organized is before age ten. If home and school do a good job in this area by age ten, school is an exciting and interesting place for children. If they do not, then school is a frustrating place which can do great damage to the child's self-view and attitude toward learning and development.

It is to be hoped that many of the IEA nations will search for ways in which to improve the curriculum and instruction in this critical area and will concern themselves especially with methods of enabling all children to profit from school by providing them the verbal tools they need to learn well and to enjoy learning.

Patterns of Objectives—Cognitive and Affective

The IEA tests have been developed to sample the content and objectives in each subject. The specifications for these evaluation procedures were provided by the national and international subject committees, and the various committees were involved in criticizing and validating the proposed evaluation instruments. In the final data processing, scores and other types of indexes have been reported for each of the cognitive and affective objectives in each subject.

Cognitive Objectives

In reading, science, literature, and mathematics, test scores in the cognitive domain have been provided at different levels of complexity, varying from direct measures of remembered knowledge or information to higher-level objectives involving complex interpretations, applications, and inferences.

In each subject, in almost every country, students perform best on the lower mental processes involving knowledge, perform less well on items involving some interpretation or comprehension, and perform least well on test problems requiring applications, higher mental processes, and complex inferences. Students in the final year of secondary education—usually the most select group in each country—do slightly better on problems involving the higher mental processes (in terms of percentage of problems correct) than do students at the fourteen-year age group.

When one looks at the emphasis in the curriculum as indicated by syllabi and curriculum experts, or when one looks at the "opportunity to learn" as judged by teachers, it is evident that the pattern of decreasing scores from lower to higher mental processes reflects these emphases. Schools, teachers, and textbooks throughout the world are apparently largely directed toward filling a presumably "empty head" with things to be remembered. Although teachers, curriculum makers, and testers profess more complex objectives for education, the actual emphasis in the classrooms is still largely on the learning of specific information.

Education throughout the world is primarily concerned with the acquisition of information or the development of literal comprehension. While there is no doubt that such "lower mental processes" are of value, it is likely that increasingly throughout the world problem solving, inferential thinking, and various higher mental processes will be required if the student is to use what he learned in the school, if school learning is to be relevant to the problems individuals encounter, and if adults are to continue learning after the school years. These objectives are basic to some of the exciting ideas about education and the learning society developed in the UNESCO report *Learning to Be.*[9]

Textbook writers and curriculum makers find it easiest to make instructional materials and curricula that emphasize lower-level cognitive processes. Testers find it easiest to design evaluation instruments that deal with factual knowledge and literal interpretation. However, the numbers of curriculum makers and evaluation specialists in each country are relatively small. The training of these specialists to make learning materials and evaluation procedures directed at more complex cognitive processes should not be difficult.

The real problem in every country is how to provide preservice and in-service education for teachers in inquiry skills, problem solving, and higher mental processes. Little progress in developing these higher processes in the schools can be expected until teachers develop the necessary capabilities and are helped to find ways of teaching higher intellectual processes to the students in their classes.

Affective Objectives

In the IEA studies there was an attempt to secure evidence on such affective objectives as interest in the subject and attitudes toward the subject, school, and school learning. In each country there is a significant correlation between measures of the affective and cognitive objectives. For example, within each country interest in science and positive attitudes toward it are significantly related to cognitive achievement in science, and the number of hours spent reading for pleasure each week (as reported by students) is highly related to reading comprehension as well as to cognitive abilities in literature.

The scores on these measures of interest and positive attitude toward the subject and toward schooling increase from ages fourteen to eighteen in most countries. But it is not clear whether there is actual growth in these affective characteristics or whether the differences are attributable to selective policies.

The evidence collected in the IEA studies and other research summaries[10] suggests that the affective objectives are largely being developed as a by-product of the cognitive objectives. That is, students who master the cognitive objectives well develop positive interests and attitudes in the subject. Students who believe they are succeeding in school come to like school. Similarly, students who believe they are learning less well than their peers tend to develop negative affect toward school subjects and toward school. Research further indicates that the affective characteristics are more closely related to the students' perception of their standing relative to their peers within a particular school than to their measured progress on standard tests given on a national or international basis.

The affective domain has been given least emphasis throughout the world by curriculum makers, teachers, or the schools. Perhaps our limited knowledge of how to develop these qualities inhibits curriculum makers and teachers from dealing directly with them. For some time to come, we can expect these affective objectives to be developed by sheer exposure to the subject matter and by accidental forces—other than the student's tendency to like things that he does well. But it is likely that reading habits, interest (and disinterest) in particular subjects, and positive as well as negative attitudes toward school and school learning may became more stable characteristics of the individual in the long run than the cognitive abilities and capabilities developed by appropriate learning experiences. If individuals are to continue learning in the major subject fields and areas of interest introduced by schools, much will depend on the affective qualities that schools have developed in them, whether they were developed intentionally or not. This is an area that warrants cooperative research throughout the world.

The Most Able Students—and the Others

If only the developed nations in the IEA are considered, it will be found that on most of the subject tests, the top 5 percent of students across the world are roughly equal in their achievement at age fourteen and at the final year of secondary education. This will generally be true whether one is considering the upper 5 percent of the entire age group sampled—such as the fourteen-year level where typically 90 percent or more of the students are still in school—or the approximations to the top 5 percent of the age group at the final year of secondary education where the countries differ widely in the percent of the age group still in school (from 9 percent in one country to 75 percent in another country).

Thus, in spite of differences in curriculum, instructional procedures, and many other differences between countries, it appears that the upper 5 percent of students in these countries are roughly comparable in their achievement as measured by these tests.

While the IEA does not provide precise data on these points, the relationships among the different variables studied suggest that these top students typically come from homes in which the parents have had a relatively high level of education (for the country), provide a great deal of interest in and support for learning in school, provide support and incentives for the development of verbal ability and reading skill, and share with their children expectations for tertiary education and entry into a learned profession.

These are students who typically have a high level of verbal ability, including word knowledge and reading comprehension, and who have had the maximum amount of years of study in each of the academic subjects. They tend to have the most favorable interests and attitudes toward the subject and positive attitudes toward school and school learning.

If education had to deal only with this small group of students, the schools could do little wrong. Even when the curriculum is inadequate or outdated and teachers provide only mediocre instruction, these students would do well. What school cannot provide, many parents would. What teachers or parents cannot provide, these students could provide for themselves. One can wax eloquent about the learning achievements of such students when aided by schools and parents—or in spite of schools and parents—but this is hardly the group that the schools are supported to serve.

In principle, the resources of at least the highly developed nations are intended to support the education of all youth—not just the top 5 or 10 percent of students and not just the children of the best-educated and most-favored citizens.

Countries differ in their treatment of students below the top 5 or 10 percent of the group. In most countries in the IEA studies a high proportion of the remaining 90 pecent are dropped from school somewhere between ages fourteen and eighteen. In spite of differences in retention of students in school there is considerable evidence that very few countries do an "adequate" educational job for the majority of this age group—and especially for the lower 50 percent of students.

What are the implications for the schools if nations are to serve more adequately the entire population of youth rather than only the top students who survive relatively well because of or in spite of the schools as they are now? If we sketch a picture based on the bottom half of students, several suggestions may be made.

Characteristically these students are drawn from the part of the population with the least-favorable conditions for education in their homes. Their parents have had less education and typically are in the lower half of occupational and income distributions. There is less support for education in the home in terms of parent interest, books, or incentives to further education. These are students with the lowest verbal ability and least-adequate reading comprehension. They spend less time in reading on their own. They do not have positive attitudes toward school, and their interests in particular academic subjects are not high. They receive few favorable rewards and reinforcements in school from their learning, from their teachers, or even from their peers.

With this group of students, the school is largely on its own and must provide for instruction without counting on the home to provide supplementary instruction or to aid the student when he is having difficulty in school. If homework is required (and the IEA studies find this to be a variable favorable for learning), the school will need to provide conditions for it to be done in school with aides or teachers to provide help when these students are having difficulty.

These students are in special need of verbal education in the preschool years or in the primary period of schooling if they are to survive in schools as now organized. Schools must also provide the models of learning and incentives for education and learning—without counting on the home to do this. Such models might be provided if teachers were able to develop closer relations with their students and encouraged and helped them when needed.

One might also hope that teachers would develop instructional strategies designed to help most of the students achieve mastery of at least the tool skills and the required subjects. Some strategies have already been experimented with in a number of countries and characteristically have enabled about four-fifths of students to do as well as the upper one-fifth of students under more conventional approaches to instruction.[11] These instructional strategies make use of the existing curriculum, but provide frequent feedback to students on their learning development or learning problems and follow the feedback with changes in instructional procedures and with help and correctives as needed. Such approaches might be expected to be less and less necessary as students gain confidence in their own learning capabilities and as they find ways of correcting their own difficulties.

Under present conditions in most countries, students become less and less interested in school learning as they find themselves doing relatively poorly and as they are frustrated by their difficulties. It is likely that some parts of the curriculum are difficult to relate to the life they lead outside school, and little of the curriculum relates to the expectations they have for work and adult life.

Curriculum makers have rarely had this group of students in mind as they attempted to formulate the specifications for the curriculum or the learning materials to be used in instruction. One might hope that in the future curriculum makers in each country would attempt to deal more directly with the learning of this group of students. National curriculum centers could profit greatly from an exchange of experiences and approaches with other nations on this problem.

**IEA and the Future for Curriculum
and Instruction**

The IEA studies provide a glimpse of education in a large number of countries. While the emphasis is on the evaluation of student learning in each subject, the variety of data on the countries, the schools, the teachers, the students, and the students' home background provides the richest store of information on education that has ever been assembled. No one of us is fully capable of determining the many ways in which these data should be analyzed and reanalyzed. It is to be hoped that scholars will become acquainted with the IEA data banks and the many possibilities for further investigation which they offer.

But educators throughout the world cannot wait for future reanalyses. They must act now on what they believe to be important and true, aided by whatever data they can assemble on the problems they regard as central. The IEA national reports will provide some of the data that policy makers, educational leaders, and teachers need. Since these reports are being written by educational research workers who are thoroughly familiar with their own national scene, it is to be hoped that interaction will be generated between educators and the IEA findings within each country and that these findings will serve as a basis for a constructive response to some of the educational problems posed by the evidence in that country.

An important new educational asset in many IEA countries is the availability of a small group of persons highly trained in educational evaluation, educational research methods, and data gathering and analysis procedures. This means that educators can try a variety of new approaches to curriculum and instruction on a pilot basis and determine which are most promising. They can investigate the most successful approaches on a broader scale and at each step can appraise the effectiveness and consequences of this work. If educators will utilize the talents and methods at present available in each of the national research centers, they can move ahead with greater confidence that they are moving in the right direction. Furthermore, the network of communication provided by the IEA and other international agencies makes it possible for each country to learn from the errors and the successes of others. While each country cannot use the work of other countries directly, it can learn from the experiences, ideas, materials, and persons available throughout the world. Each country, school, teacher, and student is unique, but all can learn from the experiences of others.

In my efforts to learn from a decade and a half of experience with the IEA methods, data, and findings, I have attempted to point up some of the more obvious findings and their implications for curriculum and instruction. These implications are little more than suggestions of what appear to me to be constructive responses to this rich store of educational data.

The least costly of these suggestions in terms of time, resources, and change to the educational system is the use of mass media such as radio, television, films, and tapes to enable a country to utilize its best teachers and teaching to supplement what thousands of teachers can at present do for their students. Such efforts can be tried on a small scale and evaluated and improved before they are tried on a larger scale.

Slightly more costly is the development of teaching-learning strategies which use existing curriculum and instructional methods and materials but which, in some countries, have enabled larger proportions of students to learn effectively. The special virtues of such teaching-learning strategies is that their effectiveness can be determined in months (rather than years), and they require a minimum of change in the teachers, the teaching, or the curriculum. Such strategies have already been applied to reading comprehension, mathematics, science, second language, and many other subjects in the school program.

Much more costly is the improvement of teaching through changes in preservice and in-service education. Such efforts should, wherever possible, make use of what other countries have learned about the least effective and most effective approaches to these problems. Effort and resources spent on such problems do not automatically yield good results. Far from it, many of the approaches already tried have produced very little, and only a few approaches appear to be promising.

Even more costly are major curriculum reforms. While such reforms may be necessary and even required by local conditions, they depend on the availability of highly trained, creative workers who use appropriate evidence and research at each step to ensure that the new is really an improvement over what it is to replace. They also depend on a thorough retraining of existing teaching personnel.

We have learned from the IEA data as well as from other research throughout the world that the curriculum and instruction provided by the home are in many ways related to the curriculum and instruction provided by the school. The largest problem each country faces is to understand how these two educational forces may best relate to each other if the education of each child is to be in his best interests as well as in society's best interests. The problem is even more complex in that it involves the school as one subsystem of a society. No longer can we think of the system of schooling as relatively insulated from other parts of the society. In the future, the schools of most nations will be under pressure to relate more clearly to the other parts of the social system. We will increasingly try to determine what can best be learned in the schools, what can best be learned elsewhere, and what can be learned only through an effective inter-relation of different parts of the social system. This is the grand vision of Edgar Faure's UNESCO report.[12] Its implementation will involve all of us in education for many years to come.

Notes

1. The centers are located in Australia, Belgium, Chile, England, the Federal Republic of Germany, Finland, France, Hungary, India, Iran, Ireland, Israel, Italy, Japan, the Netherlands, New Zealand, Poland, Rumania, Scotland, Sweden, Thailand, and the United States.

2. The US national report is being prepared by Richard M. Wolf of Teachers College, Columbia University, New York.

3. C. E. Beeby, *The Quality of Education in Developing Countries* (Cambridge, Mass.: Harvard University Press, 1966).

4. Robert L. Thorndike, *Reading Comprehension Education in Fifteen Countries: An Empirical Study*, International Studies in Evaluation, Vol. III (New York: John Wiley; Stockholm: Almqvist & Wiksell, 1973).

5. E. Kuno Beller, "Research on Organized Programs of Early Education," in *Second Handbook of Research on Teaching*, ed. Robert M. W. Travers (Chicago: Rand McNally, 1973).

6. James S. Coleman *et al.*, *Equality of Educational Opportunity* (Washington, D. C.: Government Printing Office, 1966).

7. Lady Beatrice Plowden *et al.*, *A Report of the Central Advisory Committee on Children and Their Primary Schools* (London: Her Majesty's Stationery Office, 1967).

8. R. H. Dave, "The Identification and Measurement of Environmental Process Variables That Are Related to Educational Achievement," doctoral dissertation, University of Chicago, 1963; Richard Wolf, "The Measurement of Environ-

ments," in *Testing Problems in Perspective*, ed. A. Anastasi (Washington, D. C.: American Council on Education, 1966).

    9. Edgar Faure *et al.*, *Learning to Be* (Paris: UNESCO; London: Harrap, 1972).

    10. S. B. Khan and Joel Weiss, "The Teaching of Affective Responses," in Travers, *op. cit.*

    11. *Mastery Learning: Theory and Practice*, ed. James H. Block (New York: Holt, Rinehart & Winston, 1971).

    12. Faure *et al.*, *op. cit.*

Commentary I

Endre Ballér

This commentary will be devoted primarily to some implications of the IEA findings for curriculum reform in Hungary as a particular case in point. If we draw overall implications for curriculum and instruction from the results of the IEA surveys, we are in fact immediately in the domain of educational policy, as curriculum can rightly be regarded as the very heart of education and instruction.

As Hungary is now facing a curriculum reform intended to pave the way for education in the new millennium, educational policy makers are giving special attention to the strategy and substance of curriculum development. Thus in this response I shall attempt to take into account the IEA findings with respect to some aspects of curriculum reform in Hungary.

Professor Bloom lays great emphasis on the national reports. It is undeniable that international comparisons are important, but the IEA findings cannot be used without profound and many-sided national examination. International data can be regarded as background for the national results, which focus attention on the most striking facts—tendencies (either similar or dissimilar) toward the outcomes of national analyses. The national report makes the whole survey relevant.

Additional restrictions should be pointed out here. Apart from the IEA results, other available experiences, data, and inquiries have to be taken into consideration. But, even then, policy implications cannot be inferred directly from any research, as other fundamental factors (such as the social system, its ideology, traditions, and financial resources) play the leading role.

Our national report is a thick volume of over 700 pages, minus the appendixes. The following topics are covered there: school policy and educational research; procedures and methodology; results of the cognitive tests (science and reading comprehension); noncognitive (attitude) scales; environmental factors related to achievements in learning; the organization of education and instruction and the general school and its environment; condition, role, and the work of teachers; main findings of the regression analyses; comparative evaluation of the Hungarian school system; former secondary school students in higher education—a follow-up study; and headmasters' views of the IEA survey.

Some aspects of the results have already been dealt with in periodicals, booklets, or at conferences. These facts may indicate that the IEA study is being investigated carefully both from the point of view of educational policy decisions and curriculum construction.

So far it seems that the IEA results could well contribute to the approach and solution of the following curriculum problems.

Stating Instructional Objectives

A few examples may clarify this point. The Hungarian students did fairly well on science. But if we consider that they performed relatively low on the higher mental processes or on the practical items, and if we realize that these kinds of objectives are only vaguely represented in our present curricula, we come to the conclusion that instructional objectives in the curricula should deal more with the complex processes.

The same inference can be drawn from the scores in reading comprehension. Hungarian students' relatively low achievement in reading caused us great concern. The regression analyses made it clear that home background is the greatest source of variance both between students and schools. This means that individual sociocultural handicaps are intensified by the unequal services given in the schools. We realized that our general school curriculum is unambitious and obscure in its reading objectives, which may be one of the reasons why our students did so poorly on the IEA tests.

Another way of using the IEA results in Hungary is described in Postlethwaite's paper. By checking the extent to which the pupils' performance matches the global and detailed objectives stated in the curricula, useful feedback can be obtained for curriculum developers.

Improving the Methods of Evaluating the Attainment of Educational and Instructional Objectives

The IEA survey offers an immensely rich mine of information regarding adequate procedures of evaluating objectives. This holds true even if we take into consideration the lessons to be drawn from the vulnerable points or shortcomings of the study. It is regrettable, for instance, that the methods of evaluating certain attitudes and noncognitive objectives in the IEA survey fell very short of our expectations and needs. But the IEA study showed evaluation procedures in action, and, as this is one of our main concerns in connection with curriculum reform, it is only natural that we appreciate highly this feature of the IEA enterprise.

Helping to Define Clusters of Content for the Curriculum

Some examples again are helpful. A detailed examination was undertaken of the extent to which items in science are covered in the Hungarian school curricula, and how thoroughly these topics were taught. Examination of the ratios of covered and noncovered items over populations suggests that there is an increasing overlap between the Hungarian curricula and the topics covered in the IEA tests. The low ratio of covered and noncovered items for Population I can, however, be interpreted as a rough indicator of the poor selection of topics to be taught at that level. The much higher ratios of the Hungarian science curricula for Populations II and IV suggest, on the other hand, that curricula at this level are more up to date. A further analysis of items, carried out by Dr. Zoltan Bathory, proved that the difference in the level of difficulty of items covered and those not covered in the curriculum is strikingly small. This may indicate that, apart from the discrepancy between teaching efforts and learning outcomes in our science teaching, we now devote insufficient attention to the effect of the "latent curriculum."

Strengthening the Curricular Foundations of Permanent Education

We regard the development of reading skills and habits as one of the main factors and most important tools for providing lifelong education. By means of different analyses of texts (in the light of the IEA reading comprehension tests) we found that the compulsory reading material used in our textbooks is not only very simple, compared with that encountered out of school, but also remains very simple throughout the eight years of compulsory education. This implies that there is an increasing gap between the reading material used in the textbooks at school and that used when one is reading for pleasure or for self-instruction. Our present curriculum, furthermore, does not stress the most important comprehensive objectives of reading in the elementary grades of our general school. By analyzing the IEA data we drew the following conclusions: First, more emphasis should be given to silent reading and reading speed, which are closely connected with reading comprehension. Second, the teaching of reading skills should not end in the fourth grade. Third, reading objectives ought to be defined for the fifth through the eighth grades, with emphasis on the cognitive aspect of reading in most of the subjects.

Enforcing the Mastery Learning Concept and Increasing the Leveling Effect of the School by Means of the "Open Access" Curriculum

In our national report we worked out an index of the yield of our school system. The standardized scores of means and standard deviations of the test achievements were related to the data on retentivity. Then the figures were compared with other indexes of educational expenditure as percent of GNP, certain employment ratios, and the extent of adult education. Though we are generally satisfied with the performance of the Hungarian students, the analysis of these data indicates the need for curriculum development and innovation, even if we must regard the findings with the greatest possible caution. For example, it seems that in teaching science the correct strategy is to improve effectiveness by intensive means, such as independent activity of the pupils and practical experiments, instead of strengthening "extensive factors," such as allocation of time.

In light of the data the results of the biology tests were the most encouraging. In recent years a new biology curriculum has been developed for the upper grades of our general school, which breaks with the information-centered science teaching traditions and thus leaves more time for the development of higher cognitive skills. This curriculum integrates the students' out-of-school activities much better than did the former one.

Reference was made earlier to the importance of reading skills, speed, and comprehension. Hungary is the only country among the IEA participants where achievements of the same pupils are consistently lower in reading comprehension than in science in all the three populations. Since the discriminating effect of home environment makes itself felt (especially in the earlier years) mostly through differences in reading skill and comprehension, it is necessary to increase the influence of school on improving the reading of the pupils so as to avoid undesirable selection and dropout.

It should be mentioned, finally, that the retentivity patterns in Hungary lead to the conclusion that it is desirable to extend our secondary education gradually, mainly by raising the standard of our schools in the realm of vocational skills and by offering more variations for adult education. General school education must at the same time continue its leading role. Parallel to these, special attention should be given to the most able pupils. It goes without saying that all these strategies have profound curricular implications.

Coordinating the Curricula of the Different Types of Schools

The so-called "anchor" items and other sources of information in the IEA survey indicate the increment from one population level to another. In this way we may have better insight into the problems of curriculum coordination between the general school and the three branches of our secondary schools—grammar school, technical secondary school, and schools for vocational skills—as well as adult education and extra curricular forces. The improved performance of the Hungarian students (as they pass on to the fourteen-year-old level and to the terminal year of secondary education) from Population I to Population II is the greatest of all the participating countries, whereas the growth from Population II to Population IV is the smallest. This phenomenon suggests a need for more curriculum coordination to improve the performance of students after the compulsory years while increasing holding power and improving articulation between the various types of schools.

Commentary II

Ralph W. Tyler

Professor Bloom has produced a masterful synthesis of the IEA findings and has presented thoughtful and practicable suggestions for their use in improving the educational programs of the participating countries. Dr. Ballér's paper furnishes excellent illustrations of the way in which Hungary is utilizing its IEA data to reform the national curriculum. My own experience as a seminar leader at the IEA seminar in Gränna, Sweden, leads me to appreciate the extent to which the cooperating nations are seeking to use data from the IEA project as one guide in focusing efforts toward improving curricula. Though I can add little to these fine papers, I do want to comment further on the importance of each nation's clarifying its particular conditions in order to use IEA data constructively.

One matter for clarification is the specific function of the nation's schools in relation to out-of-school experience in providing education. In most, if not all societies, children and youth learn more of the behavior important for constructive participation in the society outside of school than within. This fact does not diminish the importance of the school, but underlines the nation's dependence on the home, the working place, community institutions, peer groups, and other informal experiences to furnish a major part of the education required for a child to be successfully inducted into society. Only by clear recognition of the school's special responsibility can it be highly effective in educating its students. The distribution of educational responsibility will vary among nations because they are in different stages of economic development and have different political philosophies and structures and different social arrangements.

When reviewing the test results in various subject-matter fields, educators must have clearly in mind what the function or functions of that field is in the schools of the nation. Among the functions emphasized in various schools throughout the world are the following:

To produce scholars or career specialists in that field. In some countries, for example, science is taught in the secondary school primarily as part of the educational preparation of scientists.

Students are chosen on the basis of their promise in scientific careers, and those who are most successful in mastering the science taught in the secondary school are encouraged to continue with advanced courses in the field.

To furnish necessary or helpful training for persons who are specializing in other fields. Mathematics, for example, is sometimes offered primarily to furnish useful tools for the prospective scientist or engineer.

To provide students who are not to be specialists in the field with resources on which they can draw in dealing with problems and in enriching their lives. Mathematics furnishes a way by which nonspecialists can compute the costs of products they wish to buy. Literature offers views of social situations that enable one to see his life in perspective; reading opens a world far beyond the limitations of one's own direct experience and helps him to recognize alternative courses of action not previously perceived.

To provide an example of a society that approximates the nation's ideal. Social studies or citizenship is likely to be a subject used by some nations to help students understand and appreciate the ideal society toward which the nation is striving.

To furnish a language that enables students to communicate widely. Even the native language of children is often only partly sufficient to communicate with people throughout the nation. Students need to gain a larger working vocabulary, a greater comprehension of different language structures, and sufficient practice in more varied uses of language in order to communicate adequately in the larger society. Furthermore, a second language is commonly offered where the needs for communication are inadequately met by the students' native language.

To provide students with a common cognitive map of the important areas of life so that intellectual communities are possible. Primitive people have maps in their minds that are very different from those of people schooled in modern science. Among the primitive, for example, health and disease are viewed as rewards or punishments of supernatural forces, while the scientifically sophisticated see the healthy person as eating a nutritious diet, maintaining a regimen of exercise and rest, and avoiding disease-producing organisms. The differences in these maps make cooperative action largely impossible; even intelligent discussion is thwarted. Hence, in some countries the emphasis is on using school subjects to help students acquire cognitive maps that view important phenomena in common terms.

To develop respect for scientific and scholarly enterprise. In some societies, devotion to folklore and folk wisdom creates an environment unfavorable to the development of science and scholarship. Some nations place upon schools the responsibility for helping students understand and appreciate the contributions to society that have resulted from the development of the several fields of subject matter.

These seven are not all the possible functions a subject may serve in the school curriculum, but they are among those most frequently found, and they illustrate that the importance or even the relevance of a certain test question depends upon the function that the subject-matter field is expected to serve in a particular country. For example, a test item that represents behavior important to the scholar may be almost irrelevant to the nonspecialist who seeks guidance and light for his daily life, while another question may be an excellent example of the use of the subject by a nonspecialist. Or a test exercise that requires the student to recognize ideals that are highly significant in one nation may be of lesser concern in another. All test questions can, in general, be classified for a particular nation as representing something students may learn that is: highly important for the nation; of some importance; of no importance; irrelevant, depending on the educational function in that nation of the subject field.

A third consideration for each nation as it reviews the IEA results is the likelihood of learning in its schools the particular behavior tested. From our knowledge of how students learn we realize that certain conditions are essential to learning a particular way of thinking, feeling, or acting, or, if not essential, that they are at least supportive of effective learning. These are motivation, perception of what is to be learned, opportunity to try and practice the behavior, reinforcement, feedback on learning performance, opportunity to try and practice another approach when the first is unsuccessful, and transfer. If the schools are not generally able to arouse the interest and effort in their students to try to learn what a subject offers, successful achievement is unlikely. If the schools are unable to present clear examples of what the student is expected to learn, his efforts will lack a sense of direction, and successful achievement is unlikely.

If the schools cannot provide him with opportunities to try the behavior he is expected to learn and ample chance to practice it, successful achievement is unlikely. If the schools do not find means by which students gain satisfaction when they are learning the behavior, successful achievement is unlikely. If the schools do not furnish students who are unsuccessful in their learning tasks with information that will guide and encourage further efforts, it is unlikely that a large percent of students will be successful. If the schools do not provide students alternative approaches when they are unsuccessful with a first approach, a number of students are likely to fail in this achievement. If the schools do not provide opportunity for the students to practice outside of school what they are learning in school, little transfer is likely to take place. When the national results on the IEA tests are reviewed, it is helpful to examine these conditions for learning as well as the objectives and content of the curriculum to identify when improvements are needed.

The education of teachers is also an important topic for discussion. Greater command of subject matter is commonly suggested as a way to improve the performance of teachers. This is also a matter that can properly vary among the nations. A first consideration should be a clarification of the teacher's role at different levels of schooling. In some countries the teacher in the primary school has a major role in relating the school to the home so that the child perceives school learning as a natural extension of his learning in the home. The teacher at that level may not be expected to be a scholar or scientist but a person helpful in stimulating and guiding the children. On the other hand, the secondary school teacher in some countries exemplifies scholarship and serves as a model for the academically oriented student to emulate. Where there are differences of this sort in the role of the teacher, recruitment and preparation should be directed toward developing teachers who can perform the educational function effectively. Hence, it is not likely that a single set of recommendations regarding the improvement of the preparation of teachers will be appropriate for all nations.

In conclusion, I agree with Professor Bloom and Dr. Ballér that the IEA project can stimulate each nation to examine its curriculum critically and can furnish guidance in curriculum development. I believe, however, that the IEA results can be used most effectively when related to the conditions under which the school operates in each country.

4. The Relation of School Achievement to Differences in the Backgrounds of Children

Robert L. Thorndike

If any one fact has emerged consistently from the IEA studies it is that educational achievement is related to a variety of factors in the home backgrounds of children. This is true so far as differences in the achievements of single students within a country are concerned; it is also true so far as mean score for different countries is concerned. Several questions can be posed with respect to these relationships. First, how substantial are the relationships, both within and between countries? Are they merely statistically significant, or are they of a size that has practical significance? Second, how stable are the relationships from subject matter to subject matter and from country to country? Are the factors that receive the most weight as predictors of reading the same as the ones that receive the most weight for prediction of science or of literature? Are the factors that are most predictive in the United States also most predictive in England or Iran or Chile? If not, what reasonable explanation can be offered for the differences? Third, are the factors that are most predictive of individual differences also the most predictive of national differences? If not, what reasonable explanation can be offered for the differences?

As a partial answer to the first question, Table 4-1 shows the correlations over all countries for a number of home and community variables. Correlations are shown with scores in reading comprehension, science, and literature tests for groups of ten-year-olds, fourteen-year-olds, and students at the end of secondary school. Table 4-2 shows, in addition, the correlation for a weighted composite of the more predictive of these variables for each country taken separately. Table 4-1 shows which of the elements of home background taken singly showed some appreciable correlation with the measures of achievement. Table 4-2 shows how much of a prediction was possible from composites of the variables and how uniform the relationship was from country to country.

The median correlations in Table 4-1 are, in general, quite low. The two most predictive single items of information are father's occupation and number of books in the home, with correlations in the .20s for ten-year-olds and fourteen-year-olds, but smaller at the end of secondary school. Other items show even smaller correlations. Why are the relationships no more substantial than this? There are at least three main contributing factors. One relates to the crudeness of the data. Information was obtained from pupils by questionnaire and was typically reported in no more than five response categories. These categories were chosen so as to be most effective over the whole range of countries being studied. Thus, the question on books in the home read,

About how many books are there in your home? (Do not count newspapers or magazines.) (Choose one.)
   A. None
   B. 1-10 books
   C. 11-25 books
   D. 26-50 books
   E. 51 or more books

To show some of the problems of using a questionnaire item such as this internationally, the proportions of responses are shown in Table 4-3 for fourteen-year-olds in India and Sweden.

Although the five response categories serve to emphasize the difference between India and Sweden in home circumstances, they are not well chosen to differentiate the size of home libraries in Sweden. Over 70 percent of the responses fall in a single category. Under the circumstances, the correlation of .27 found for Sweden should,

Table 4-1

Median correlations across countries of background factors
and individual achievement (decimal points omitted)

Background factors	Reading comprehension Age group			Science Age group			Literature Age group	
	10	14	18	10	14	18	14	18
Father's occupation	28	29	11	23	23	09	-	-
Father's education	-[a]	20	17	-	17	10	17	12
Mother's education	-	19	13	-	15	08	15	12
Books in home	25	27	13	23	21	09	23	13
Magazines in home	-	14	08	-	06	07	14	08
Use of dictionary	11	10	06	09	09	-02	10	09
Family size	-14	-14	-02	-12	-10	-02	-12	-04
Sex of student	02	02	05	-11	-20	-30	21	18
Parents help with homework	-03	-08	-06	-06	-11	-07	-06	-05
Parents correct spelling	06	02	-03	04	-01	-05	00	01
Parents correct writing	01	01	-02	00	00	-01	04	03
Encouraged to read	06	07	04	06	05	-06	07	07
Interested in school	08	10	-01	07	05	-06	07	06
Encouraged to visit museums	-	05	05	-	03	04	07	06

[a]Data not available.

perhaps, be considered surprisingly high. Many items involved groupings at least as coarse as the one illustrated.

Or consider the coding of father's occupation. The basic datum
was the pupil's response to the instruction:

Please write your father's occupation. On the lines below, describe his occupation as clearly as you can.

From the pupil's statement a coder assigned the occupation to one of
not more than nine categories. The categories were specified by each
national center in terms that made sense for that country. In the
United States the categories were: 9—professional, technical, and
kindred workers; 8—managers, officials, and proprietors, including
farm owners and managers; 7—white-collar workers; 6—skilled
manual workers; 5—semiskilled workers; 4—farm workers, fishery,
forestry, and kindred groups; 3—domestic and personal service
workers; 2—laborers; 1—unclassifiable; 0—unknown.

Table 4-2
Composite prediction in each country and population
(decimal points in correlations omitted)

Country	Reading comprehension versus background composite Age group			Science versus home circumstances Age group			Literature versus home background Age group	
	10	14	18	10	14	18	14	18
Australia	-[a]	-	-	-	33	11	-	-
Belgium (Flemish)	27	32	34	16	15	-	15	17
Belgium (French)	40	33	22	30	-	-	26	07
Chile	14	42	32	13	26	29	30	21
England	44	53	15	41	45	-02	36	07
Federal Republic of Germany	-	-	-	20	31	01	-	-
Finland	38	48	13	23	34	10	30	06
France	-	-	-	-	-	06	-	-
Hungary	45	47	29	25	31	22	-	-
India	15	18	16	07	15	18	-	-
Iran	38	23	22	19	17	09	20	20
Israel	54	54	30	-	-	-	-	-
Italy	31	33	27	18	16	17	21	20
Japan	-	-	-	33	38	-	-	-
Netherlands	35	37	15	30	27	08	-	-
New Zealand	-	41	20	-	33	07	25	08
Scotland	46	51	23	42	48	14	-	-
Sweden	30	41	27	27	28	13	21	11
Thailand	-	-	-	-	31	-	-	-
United States	42	51	46	40	41	31	32	27

[a]Data not available.

Scale values were empirically determined for each of the categories so as to maximize the correlation of the scaled variable with achievement. The basic categories were chosen, however, more in terms of their demographic than of their psychometric relevance. Furthermore, coding was based on the limited and sometimes ambiguous information supplied by the pupil. The fact that an "Unclassifiable" category was required and was used for 13.6 percent of the ten-year-olds, 8.1 percent of the fourteen-year-olds and 6.4 percent at the end of secondary education in the United States serves to document the difficulty that coders experienced in working with the information

Table 4-3
Percent of fourteen-year-olds checking each response to the item
on books in the home

Response	Percent	
	India	Sweden
A (None)	11.9	0.9
B (1-10 books)	35.9	2.0
C (11-25 books)	22.5	7.0
D (26-50 books)	12.3	18.3
E (51 or more books)	17.4	71.8

obtained from the questionnaire. Even so, in the United States the correlation for this scaled variable was .33 for ten-year-olds and .29 for both fourteen-year-olds and for high school seniors.

The second main attenuation in relationships may stem from incorrect information reported by pupils, especially by the ten-year-olds. Some preliminary work was done to determine the dependability of information reported in questionnaires by checking student reports against information gathered from direct contact with parents or from school records. The agreement was good enough to encourage the project to continue to rely upon pupils as the basic source of information about home and family circumstances. But, of course, the agreement was not perfect. And most of the pilot studies were done in developed countries with a relatively high standard of literacy. One must question whether the findings of these studies apply in developing countries where the average level of reading achievement is, as our surveys have indicated, much lower. It was in these developing countries, where the questionnaire items must have presented a very difficult reading task for many young people, that the correlations were lowest.

The third point to be mentioned is that each of the variables represents a specific, limited, and somewhat indirect indicator of the total environment in which the child has grown up. Books represent one resource for intellectual stimulation of the child, but magazines, newspapers, radio, and television represent additional channels for intellectual stimulation. And sheer numbers of books tell nothing about the appropriateness of the books to a child or, in fact, what sorts of books are present, or whether anyone ever reads them.

If the indicators are individually of only modest power as predictors of achievement, how powerful are they as a team? This is the problem to which Table 4-2 provides some answer. The correlations here are for a composite home background variable, but the composite was somewhat differently arrived at for the three subject areas. In particular, items relating to reading resources in the home were excluded and treated separately in the literature analyses, whereas they were included for the other two subjects. In general, in the composite variable, component background factors were so weighted as to maximize the correlations of the composite with the achievement measure.

We now see correlations running as high as .54, although the typical joint prediction falls somewhere in the .30s. The range of correlations is quite large. How are we to interpret this?

Note first that the correlations are typically much lower at the end of secondary school. In most countries the group still in school at the end of secondary school is quite select—anywhere from 10 to 25 percent of the age group, the remainder having already dropped out. Selectivity has operated on the basis of some combination of academic competence and socioeconomic status. Most of those from the lower socioeconomic groups have dropped out unless they were especially competent. Thus, the selection has operated both to reduce the range of socioeconomic status and to leave in school a nonrepresentative fraction of children from the lower socioeconomic strata. As a result, correlations almost universally dropped. The one exception is the United States, where perhaps 75 percent of the age group completes secondary school, and where socioeconomic variables appear less related to the fact of dropping out of school. In the United States the prediction of achievement for eighteen-year-olds is about as accurate as at the earlier levels.

In addition to the difference between the group composed of those who complete secondary school and the younger groups, there are notable differences between countries. Considering reading comprehension, one notes composite correlations as high as .54 in Israel, .53 in England, and .51 in Scotland and the United States, while composite correlations reach only .14 in Chile (for ten-year-olds) and .15 in India. How are those differences to be understood?

One explanation is that the countries showing the low correlations are homogeneous, that there is little variation from pupil to pupil in the socioeconomic indexes in question, and consequently that there is little opportunity for covariation to appear. This explanation can apparently be rejected. At least when we took three separate variables for fourteen-year-olds and examined the relationship between national variability (standard deviation of responses on the scaled item) and national correlation with reading comprehension score, the correlations were in each instance negative. The countries with the greater variability showed the smaller correlations. This negative value is probably not to be taken seriously, but it does at least argue against any significant positive relationship.

A second explanation asserts that in the developing countries many pupils were simply unable to read and to respond meaningfully to the student questionnaire. It became clear, as the test papers from the IEA study were processed, that many pupils in the three developing countries (Chile, India, and Iran) were responding at or close to a chance level on the reading tests. Tests that were designed to be, and in fact were, of appropriate difficulty for the typical pupil in the developed countries of Europe were clearly too difficult for children in these three countries. Since the student questionnaire was in a sense a test of reading and of following directions, and very probably as difficult as the ten-year-old version of the reading comprehension test, it seems reasonable to suppose that those who were unable to handle the reading test, responding to it in a random fashion, were also unable to handle the questionnaire and may have responded to its questions in almost a random fashion. Future investigators working with marginally literate populations may need to develop other approaches to obtaining background information about their subjects.

A third explanation, which does not exclude the previous one as a contributory factor, is that the same indicator may have genuinely different significance in different cultures. We may take number of siblings as an example. This variable showed a negative correlation with achievement in all but one of the developed countries, the Flemish-speaking area of Belgium. The correlation was positive, however, in several of the developing countries, such as India, Iran, and Thailand. Perhaps a small family signifies qualities of restraint, planning, and concern for children's education in most Western countries, but has quite different implications for developing countries in the East. As another illustration, occupational level turns out to be a much weaker predictor in such countries as India, Iran, and Thailand.

Possibly in these countries there is no clear-cut occupational hierarchy that has the same connotation of economic advantage and cultural stimulation that seems to attach to this hierarchy in the developed countries.

It is hard to judge whether such differences do exist in the basic significance of indicators until it is possible to rule out reading difficulties as a contributing factor. A future study in which information about home and family is gathered at the source, that is, from a parent, by a trained interviewer, would seem to be required if one is to reach a judgment as to the weight to be attached to the two explanatory factors.

Table 4-1 provides some evidence on the consistency of the relationship of background variables as one goes from one age level to another. Except for the fact that all correlations are lower for the eighteen-year-olds, consistency across ages and subjects seems to be the rule, and variations appear to be relatively minor. There is perhaps a suggestion that the availability of reading matter in the home is less important for science achievement than for achievement in reading and literature. It is unfortunate that no data were gathered on home variables that might have been more related to science, possibly such an item as the availability of tools and a home workshop, or having a parent who carried out a wide variety of home repairs; thus, no variables appear that show a stronger relationship to achievement in science. Sex of student is the one major exception to the consistent pattern, since boys tend to do markedly better on the science tests and girls on the literature tests. But, since both boys and girls do equally well in reading, one suspects that the sex patterns are related to factors in the larger culture and the curriculum of the schools.

There were a few surprises in the relationships that emerged, or sometimes in those that failed to emerge. One group of variables was introduced to measure the home's level of interest in schooling and the home's pressure for achievement. These were items that attempted to tap by way of questionnaires some of the aspects of the home that had been found in interview-observation studies to show a strong positive relationship to a child's achievement. There were such questions as: "How often does your mother or father help you with your homework?" "When you talk at home, do your parents insist that you speak correctly?" "When you get home from school, do your parents ask about your schoolwork?" Table 4-1 shows, however, that the correlations in this study were all small and were sometimes negative. It appears, in particular, that parents' help with homework is more an indication of childish ineptitude than of parental commitment. The correlation was negative practically without exception for all countries, all subjects, and all levels. Perhaps parental behavior as seen and reported by a pupil is quite different from parental behavior as reported by a parent or seen by an adult observer, but more likely the information obtainable by questionnaire indicates a different type or level of parental involvement than that obtained by more probing approaches.

Table 4-2 provides some evidence on the consistency of prediction through background variables as one goes from country to country. Attention has already been directed to the relatively low values in Chile, India, and Iran, and for all countries except the United States at the end of secondary school, and possible explanations for these results have been proposed. A further question might be: to what extent is a country consistently high or low in the predictability of achievement? As one answer to this, we have computed a coefficient of concordance over several of the better predictors and over the two subject areas of reading and science. Thus, for each predictor the available countries were ranked for size of correlation coefficient, both for ten-year-olds and fourteen-year-olds, and the concordance of the ranks determined. For science the coefficient of concordance was .76, and the average rank order correlation was .70; for reading the corresponding values were .81 and .78. Thus, there is substantial consistency both over predictors and over age groups in the countries in which prediction from background variables is effective. An overall ranking of thirteen countries from most to least predictable results in the following order: Scotland, England, Hungary, United States, Finland, Belgium (French), Chile, Sweden, Netherlands, Italy, Iran, Belgium (Flemish), India.

It is interesting to speculate on what accounts for this order. As previously noted, prediction was relatively poor in the developing countries, especially Iran and India, and possible reasons have been offered for this finding. Prediction is especially good in the English-speaking countries, which could reflect the fact that all the tests and questionnaires were initially developed in the English language. The tests were slightly more reliable in English-speaking countries, and it is possible that the questionnaire items were somehow clearer, leading to more precise responses. But why does Hungary fall so near the top, and why is Flemish-speaking Belgium so near the bottom?

So far we have considered background factors as predictors of the achievements of individual children. What about the prediction of between-country differences? Do national differences in the availability of books in the home, for example, correspond to national differences in achievement? Some evidence on this problem is provided in Table 4-4, where correlations are shown between average reading comprehension score and average score on each of a number of background variables. Correlations are shown with the three developing countries included, and also with these countries removed.

From Table 4-4 it is apparent that any of a number of background variables corresponds fairly well with average achievement if the three developing countries are included. When these countries are omitted, however, the correlations are generally small, and quite different variables are the best predictors. It is also true that the variables that best differentiate among countries are not the same as

Table 4-4

Correlations of country mean reading comprehension with other
national variables, Population II

Variable	All fifteen countries	Twelve developed countries
Father's education	.60	.14
Mother's education	.73	.23
Expected education	.67	.30
Hours of homework weekly	.25	.19
Hours of instruction—mother tongue	.21	.47
Parents help with homework	.53	.13
Parents encourage to read	.56	.04
Parents interested in school	.07	.12
Dictionary available	.09	.25
Number of books in home	.85	.17
Number of magazines in home	.71	.36
Hours of radio or TV	.92	.28
Frequency of movie attendance	.23	.07
Hours of reading for pleasure	.16	.29

Source: Robert L. Thorndike, *Reading Comprehension Education in Fifteen Countries*, International Studies in Evaluation, Vol. III (New York: John Wiley; Stockholm: Almqvist & Wiksell, 1973), 147.

those that best differentiate among individuals. Among the developed countries, for example, number of magazines differentiates better than number of books, whereas for individual pupils the order is quite the reverse. Again, the report that parents help with homework is a favorable indicator between countries, while between pupils within a country it is an unfavorable one. Between countries the time devoted to TV and radio is as powerful an indicator as time spent reading for pleasure; for individuals, reading time is much more predictive. It appears, therefore, that the dynamics of prediction across countries is quite different from the dynamics across individuals. One possible interpretation is that indicators of economic development are more potent across countries, whereas indicators of cultural enrichment are more potent across individuals.

In the IEA studies some attention was also paid to characteristics of schools as indicators of achievement. In those analyses it was extremely important to partial out the influence of background variables of the sorts considered in this chapter. Background factors producing correlations of around .30 between individuals yielded correlations as high as .70 when these correlations related to average input and average achievement for a school. By comparison, most school variables (that is, variables describing some aspect of schooling within a school) gave small, erratic, and inconsistent correlations from country to country. Thus, in spite of the modest correlations obtained for background variables, they seemed much more effective predictors than any of the items that described the school as an educational unit. If there had been direct measures of the children as they entered school, even higher correlations would almost certainly have been obtained between pupil input and average achievement. In many countries, including the United States, the input variables delimit rather sharply the range of outputs that it is reasonable to expect for a school. Thus, though factors related to home background provide only a rough guide to expected individual performance, they define rather sharply the expected performance of a school.

Commentary I

Ronald Edmonds

Such contacts as I have had with IEA personnel show them to be men and women of substance and merit. I am therefore doubly pained at having to take such strong exception to their ambitious undertaking. I hope it is understood, however, that my criticism is offered in a mood of amiability and cooperation in the belief that the IEA beginnings might eventually yield greater policy gain than is now the case.

The IEA inquiry in general and Professor Thorndike's work in particular confirm a portion of conventional educational wisdom that is mischievous at least and pernicious in certain of the uses to which it is put. Conventional educational wisdom, in the United States, endorses manipulation of children and their environment whenever children are judged unacceptably deviant from our ethnocentric norms. The opportunity for mischief is obvious in such a circumstance. We grow pernicious when our rationale for intervention extends to defining large groups of people as "culturally deprived" by reason of their cultural or linguistic deviation from our norms. The IEA study lends itself to such abuse.

That the IEA work confirms Coleman and similar researchers was probably predictable from the moment its overall plan was developed. That is so because these inquiries occurred within political and ideological parameters that precluded insight into certain profound questions that remain about education in general and public schooling in particular.

The IEA decided, at the outset, to seek information on pupils and learning as opposed to schools and teaching. Only one of the six "areas of inquiry" is devoted to explicit information on school characteristics. Areas of inquiry are a researcher's prerogative and ought not ordinarily be contested, but mischief occurs here because the "areas" are described as "predictors of accomplishment." That means the IEA proceeded from certain premises that coincide with the conventional wisdom I mentioned earlier. In summary, I infer those premises to be: first, educational assessment is a normative process, and the researcher can use his own judgment in establishing or ascertaining the norm; second, pupil performance on standardized measures is a reasonable indicator of academic ability and general intelligence; third, pupil characteristics both predict and delimit academic performance; and, finally and most importantly, the responsibility for educational outcomes rests primarily with pupils and their parents as opposed to schools and their teachers.

Taken together such premises predict at least two outcomes for educational assessment: schools serve pupils well or poorly in conformity to the social and economic status of the pupils; middle-class pupils are well served, and poor pupils are not.

Such an observation is not liable to contest, and our disagreement concerns, therefore, the questions to be asked in response to the predicted outcome. Let me suggest certain questions the answers to which would have unambiguous policy implications alternative to prevailing practice among most of the school systems that are a part of the IEA study. What is the relationship between pupil performance and the origin of the uses to which the school is to be put? What is the relationship between pupil performance and the school's perceptions of parents and pupils as clients, or constituents, or both? What is the relationship between pupil performance and assessment on the basis of central normative, or local criterion, measures? Is a school a social-service setting, and, if so, is pupil performance the principal responsibility of the family or the school?

I am not suggesting that the IEA inquiry could have answered such questions. I am critical because there is little to suggest that the IEA was interested in such questions. Not to be interested is a measure of the parameters of the inquiry, its reporting, and its policy implications.

The whole of the IEA inquiry is cast in a different light by altering certain of the a priori positions that inform the work. In the "General Summary" Thorndike concludes "a dominant determiner of the outcome from a school in terms of reading performance is the input in terms of the kinds of students that go to the school." Using the same data that brought Thorndike to that observation I would say that a dominant determiner of the outcome from a school in terms of reading performance is the input in terms of the school's response to the kinds of students that go to the school.

Such an alternative observation illustrates the core of our disagreement. In assessing public schooling, I place the greatest burden on the schools as opposed to the pupils.

The central question for each of us is how best to respond to the relationship between the pupil's social and economic status and his performance. The implication in the IEA work is that one must intervene in the life of the child so as to convey to him the behavior and characteristics the schools regard as prerequisite to successful performance. The data, freed from its political and ideological parameters, might well suggest that what is wanted is intervention in the life of the school so as to compel a more effective instructional response to those who profit least from prevailing arrangements.

The present study says little of how schooling might be made more equitable. Neither does it say such an effort is inappropriate or that it might not yield gains that would profit us all.

In addition to answering the questions I have already suggested, researchers must alter the inferred premises that characterize the IEA study in order to effect greater educational equity.

Educational assessment requires that the criteria to be used be defined. When a researcher feels free to use normative measures, he has established that the normative criteria are acceptable to the most powerful people in the educational community being assessed. He has also established that if these criteria do not coincide with the expectations of some pupils and their parents it will be of no consequence because such parents will be impotent in their contest of the assessment. Such authority relations are illustrative of inequitable institutional responses to heterogeneous populations. In such a context data on pupil performance that is a function of income and social class ought to give a researcher serious cause for questioning a priori assumptions about "predictors of accomplishment."

The intelligence quotient and standardized measures are further illustrative of the authority relations in schooling. Both kinds of instruments permit the researcher to define for himself what constitutes ability and intelligence. If intelligence is defined as effective functioning in a society and ability as one's proficiency at certain tasks, it is important to know the relationship between the pupil behaviors being recorded and their relationship to the aspirations and culture of the pupil and his family. Thus, the IEA instruments were more reliable when they were recording the behaviors of pupils who share and accept the norm that schooling represents in this inquiry.

Variations in the background of the pupil need not predict his performance. They may do so because schools usually share the society's inequitable and discriminatory response to the poor and others who are disadvantaged. The Welsh in England, blacks in America, and the poor everywhere illustrate the ethnocentrism that usually characterizes school response to differences that are not valued by the schools. In such a circumstance data on pupil performance must be treated carefully to avoid inferring an equity in schooling that may not exist.

The political and ideological implications of all educational assessment may be best illustrated by consideration of the social-service definition of schooling that is to be used. Data related to performance are of no help. The definition to be used is a function of one's perspective and disposition.

Schools must serve pupils and their parents. Data concerning performance thus assess the effectiveness of the school. Ineffective schools must be altered in conformity to pupil characteristics and parental expectations. It is my hope that future IEA inquiries are more explicitly directed to the tasks defined by this critique.

Commentary II

Sarane Spence Boocock

The overall impression I received from reading the three volumes on reading comprehension, literature, and science was the sameness of the results concerning the effects of family background. No matter what subject or country was being analyzed, children whose parents were themselves well educated, economically advantaged, and not burdened with large families, and whose homes contained much reading material, were more likely to perform well on the IEA tests than children without these advantages. These correlations held across all the countries in the sample, even though the sample countries represented considerable variation in political structure and ideology. The most dramatic differences in test scores are between the developed countries and the developing ones, a finding that Thorndike points out is consistent with the general relationship between achievement and background, since "the developed countries differ from the developing ones perhaps most sharply in just those characteristics that characterize the children in the developed countries who read well. That is, the developed countries are in general able to provide an environment in which the parents are educated, in which books and magazines are available, and in which the media of radio and television are accessible to all the children."[1]

The size of the correlations tended to be larger among the younger groups than among the older students in Population IV, but this is itself partly a function of background, since students still in school at the last year of secondary education are more likely to come from high-status families. (The one country that still showed a substantial correlation between achievement and background in Population IV was the United States, where the majority of youth complete high school.)

I am not sure whether the size of the correlations varies regularly across subject matter, or even whether such comparisons could be made with the IEA data. I recall seeing a study of children in the United States that showed that the variations among them were greater in reading than in mathematics, the interpretation being that the former was a skill that could more easily be nurtured in the home (most parents are at least capable of reading stories to their children; relatively few are able to play mathematical games or engage in other activities with their children that would enhance mathematical skills).

The kinds of limitations that the home background and experiences place upon the school are, I believe, captured in the "school handicap score" discussed in the volume on science education by Comber and Keeves. The purpose of this variable was to establish a kind of academic baseline so that a fair estimate of the achievement increment of a given school could be made. It says, in effect, that any school with a high proportion of students whose parents have little formal education themselves, who have a large number of children to provide for, and whose homes have few intellectual resources begins with a serious handicap in teaching these children.

There has been some question about the validity of these scores because of the correlation between the student input variables that comprise the handicap score and the school variables, whose effect on achievement is being evaluated. But the score still seems to me to birth control should, by decreasing the size of families, have a positive effect upon the academic performance of the children.)

Some of the most promising educational experiments are home intervention programs, such as the one in Jerusalem designed by Avima Lombard at the Hebrew University Center for Research in Education of the Disadvantaged to mobilize mothers to act at home as educators for their preschool children. The mothers, mostly from the lowest socioeconomic levels of Israeli society, spend twenty minutes a day, five days a week, for ten weeks, covering lessons on formal language, sensory discrimination, and problem solving with their children. An important component of the program design is that the mothers are taught how to use the materials by aides chosen from the same socioeconomic level, wherever possible from the same neighborhoods, who also recruit the mother-teachers and serve as liaison with the university-based project staff. The objective of the project is not only to improve the child's readiness for school, but also to give the mother a fresh framework for interaction with her child, which will in turn help her to a greater awareness of the child's potential and the possibilities of stimulating him further.

The notion of home intervention is tricky. It seems, among other things, to violate another of the interesting findings of the IEA studies, which is the generally negative effect of parental participation, including help with homework. Thorndike's interpretation is that such help "tends to occur in proportion to its being needed and that is the poor achiever rather than the good achiever who receives special parental help." There is, on the other hand, some scattered empirical evidence[2] that students with high grades in a given subject are likely to have received large amounts of tutorial help at home. I do not believe we are close to knowing where the line is between parental activities that enrich the child's intellectual life and those that interfere with his academic success. My best guess from the research findings I have examined is that a home socialization process that sensitizes children to adult standards and demands, but that also encourages initiative and self-reliance with respect to work (a process which, somewhat ironically, interested adults spend much time helping children to learn to work independently of them) is the most conducive to ultimate school success. By contrast, observers of ghetto classrooms, populated by children whose lives have been impoverished in terms of interaction with interested adults, report that such

describe quite accurately what schools are up against even when
are genuinely committed to raising the achievement levels of
dents. If schooling is a process that is, as Comber and Keeves
"superimposed on home and society for a limited part of the da
of life as a whole," and if students arrive at school with a
experiences and attitudes that shape their subsequent perfor
there, does this imply that strategies that focus upon raisi
quality of home and community life offer a greater rewar
further innovations in curriculum and school facilities? Whi
not believe that one can give a definite answer to this quest
me mention briefly some of the approaches suggested by the
strategy. One approach is to extend the influence of the scho
vis the home and community; it is represented by the He
program in the United States and the attempt of the Israeli
of Education to provide prekindergarten experience for all
ages three to five in immigrant villages and development tov
strategy is, of course, indirect with respect to improving hor
does not really do anything about the family, but simply
lessen the influence of family background by increasing
away from the family and in an educational setting.

A second and more direct approach provides more fam
the kinds of resources that characterize families with high
children. This is the notion behind toy libraries, which l
tional toys and games to families that cannot afford to
along with instruction in their use, and behind the Hookec
program, which distributes paperback books to children i
to. The designers of the latter program claim that owner
books raises the children's motivation to read them, an
ment for distributing learning resources in homes rather
ing school and community libraries, which tend to be use
tionately by families on a higher socioeconomic level. N
the educational and occupational levels of parents is m
though it would be an interesting experiment to see
parents with additional educational opportunities wo
raise the achievement levels of their children. (There ar
optimism in the worldwide trend toward more years of f
tion. As young people of childbearing age have even r
schooling, there should be an overall trend toward ris
performance of school-age children. Likewise, nationa

birth control should, by decreasing the size of families, have a positive effect upon the academic performance of the children.)

Some of the most promising educational experiments are home intervention programs, such as the one in Jerusalem designed by Avima Lombard at the Hebrew University Center for Research in Education of the Disadvantaged to mobilize mothers to act at home as educators for their preschool children. The mothers, mostly from the lowest socioeconomic levels of Israeli society, spend twenty minutes a day, five days a week, for ten weeks, covering lessons on formal language, sensory discrimination, and problem solving with their children. An important component of the program design is that the mothers are taught how to use the materials by aides chosen from the same socioeconomic level, wherever possible from the same neighborhoods, who also recruit the mother-teachers and serve as liaison with the university-based project staff. The objective of the project is not only to improve the child's readiness for school, but also to give the mother a fresh framework for interaction with her child, which will in turn help her to a greater awareness of the child's potential and the possibilities of stimulating him further.

The notion of home intervention is tricky. It seems, among other things, to violate another of the interesting findings of the IEA studies, which is the generally negative effect of parental participation, including help with homework. Thorndike's interpretation is that such help "tends to occur in proportion to its being needed and that it is the poor achiever rather than the good achiever who receives special parental help." There is, on the other hand, some scattered empirical evidence[2] that students with high grades in a given subject are likely to have received large amounts of tutorial help at home. I do not believe we are close to knowing where the line is between parental activities that enrich the child's intellectual life and those that interfere with his academic success. My best guess from the research findings I have examined is that a home socialization process that sensitizes children to adult standards and demands, but that also encourages initiative and self-reliance with respect to work (a process in which, somewhat ironically, interested adults spend much time helping children to learn to work independently of them) is the most conducive to ultimate school success. By contrast, observers of ghetto classrooms, populated by children whose lives have been impoverished in terms of interaction with interested adults, report that such describe quite accurately what schools are up against even when they are genuinely committed to raising the achievement levels of students. If schooling is a process that is, as Comber and Keeves put it, "superimposed on home and society for a limited part of the day and of life as a whole," and if students arrive at school with a set of experiences and attitudes that shape their subsequent performance there, does this imply that strategies that focus upon raising the quality of home and community life offer a greater reward than further innovations in curriculum and school facilities? While I do not believe that one can give a definite answer to this question, let me mention briefly some of the approaches suggested by the former strategy. One approach is to extend the influence of the school vis-à-vis the home and community; it is represented by the Head Start program in the United States and the attempt of the Israeli Ministry of Education to provide prekindergarten experience for all children ages three to five in immigrant villages and development towns. This strategy is, of course, indirect with respect to improving home life; it does not really do anything about the family, but simply tries to lessen the influence of family background by increasing the time away from the family and in an educational setting.

A second and more direct approach provides more families with the kinds of resources that characterize families with high-achieving children. This is the notion behind toy libraries, which lend educational toys and games to families that cannot afford to buy them, along with instruction in their use, and behind the Hooked-on-Books program, which distributes paperback books to children in the ghetto. The designers of the latter program claim that ownership of the books raises the children's motivation to read them, another argument for distributing learning resources in homes rather than enlarging school and community libraries, which tend to be used disproportionately by families on a higher socioeconomic level. Manipulating the educational and occupational levels of parents is more difficult, though it would be an interesting experiment to see if providing parents with additional educational opportunities would in itself raise the achievement levels of their children. (There are grounds for optimism in the worldwide trend toward more years of formal education. As young people of childbearing age have even more years of schooling, there should be an overall trend toward rise in academic performance of school-age children. Likewise, national programs of children often have an excessive dependence upon the teacher, to the point that they fail to respond to the learning materials and activities provided for them. Thus it seems to me that the most direct translation of the IEA findings on social background into educational policy or methodology would be in the form of techniques for helping parents and other adults outside the school to participate more meaningfully in their children's lives. Such techniques would focus not upon parents' "doing" their children's homework with them, but upon developing in them inquisitiveness, alertness, problem-solving skills, and confidence in their own learning capacities.

Notes

1. Robert L. Thorndike, *Reading Comprehension Education in Fifteen Countries: An Empirical Study*, International Studies in Evaluation, Vol. III (New York: John Wiley; Stockholm: Almqvist & Wiksell, 1973), 177.
2. See R. H. Dave, "The Identification and Measurement of Environmental Process Variables That Are Related to Educational Achievement," doctoral dissertation, University of Chicago, 1963.

Commentary III

Marshall S. Smith

In the following remarks I take the liberty of speaking to the broad issue of the effects of schools on learning in the context of the IEA effort. I shall begin with four general assertions and then briefly consider arguments with respect to each of them. Finally, I shall turn to some of the ways in which I believe the IEA has advanced our understanding. The four assertions are:

1. The IEA data can tell us little about the effects of school on children's achievement.

This commentary was prepared as a response to James S. Coleman's paper on school effects. Although Dr. Coleman's paper cannot be included in this volume, Dr. Smith's paper serves as a further commentary on Dr. Thorndike's paper.

2. The IEA data can tell us little about the relative magnitude of the effects of home background and schools on children; we cannot determine from them which has the greater effect on the achievement of youngsters.

3. The IEA data supply only partial information about whether schools or schooling either "open" or "close the gap" among countries or among groups within the same country.

4. The IEA data do not tell us very much about the differential effects of differences among schools. These data can only give us some weak guesses about ways of changing schools to make them more productive.

The arguments supporting these assertions are simple, and they overlap in some ways. They are stated simply because I believe that the IEA data have been badly misinterpreted in the press and other places, and I should like to try to clear up some of the confusion. Let us consider each point in turn.

The first point is that the IEA data tell us little about the effects of schools on achievement. In order to estimate the effect of any intervention such as schooling we need to determine two things. First, we must be able to measure the level of attainment of a group of children who have been exposed to the intervention for a certain amount of time. Second, we need to be able to measure the level of attainment for a similar group of children who have not been exposed to the intervention. The difference between the attainment levels of the two groups gives us an idea of the magnitude of the effect of the intervention. With few exceptions the IEA data, or almost any other data that I know of, do not allow us to estimate the magnitude of this effect because we lack the necessary comparison group of similar children who did not attend school. Schools may have a great effect or a small effect (I suspect the former), but we cannot tell from these data. In the few cases in which comparisons exist, the IEA data seem to indicate that schooling is important. The reports on both science and French as a second language, for example, indicate that the amount of time spent in course work in a subject bears a strong relation to a child's attainment in the subject. The policy implication may be obvious, but it is not trivial: if you want children to learn something about science or French as a second language, expose them to courses in science or French. Although this strategy may not work for all children, on the average it seems to have some effect. Similarly the data coming from the anchor items on the various tests suggest an important effect of schooling, although I am skeptical about interpreting items in the same way across ages. I should also note that maturation is fully confounding the school variable in this instance.

Even if we cannot say much about the effects of schools, can we say something about the relative or differential effects of home background and schooling on achievement? My second point asserts that we cannot. Once again we face the problem of the lack of control groups. Essentially we would need two samples of children from each of the variety of home backgrounds. One of the samples from each background would have attended school while the other sample did not. A design of this sort would allow us to estimate the independent effects of home background, schooling, and of interactions between home background and schooling. Lacking such a design we can say little about the question. Some might wonder about this point. After all, the Boston *Globe* indicated that one of the findings of the IEA data was that home background was a more important determinant of achievement than schooling. What the *Globe* should have said was that variation in achievement appears to be more related to variation in home background than to variation in schooling, a statement that *may* say something about equality of educational opportunity, but that says nothing about the relative effects of home background and schooling. I will try to make this distinction clear with an example. Imagine that we have an absolute measure of achievement, one that yields a score interpretable apart from normative comparisons. Suppose we administer this test to fifth-grade students of ten different levels of home background. Now imagine that students at the lowest level of home background learn something from their homes. In the context of our hypothetical test of achievement, suppose that the home background of these students contributes one point to their scores. Students who live in homes classified at the second lowest level learn something more from their home. Let us say their homes contribute two points to their scores. We can continue with this assumption until we reach the highest level of home background, where the assumed contribution is ten points. Now suppose that schooling also makes a contribution to the achievement test scores of these children. For the sake of argument, suppose that schools have a uniform effect on children of the different social classes—a large effect of, let us say, 100 points on our achievement test. Thus after we have administered our test and looked at the distribution of scores we have a range from 101 points to 110 points. We find, moreover, that home background correlates perfectly with achievement scores and that schooling has a zero correlation with achievement scores. Can we conclude from this that home background has a greater effect on achievement than schools? Of course we cannot. In this hypothetical example schooling has contributed 100 points while the most home background has contributed is ten points. This is an exaggerated example but I think it makes the point. If we look only at the relation between the variation of home background and achievement and the relation between the variation in schooling and achievement in the condition where all the children are attending school, we can say nothing about the absolute or relative magnitude of the effect of either home background or schools on the achievement of youngsters. This is, by and large, the situation with the IEA data. It is also the situation, of course, in many other cross-sectional surveys.

What then does the moderately strong correlation between home background and achievement at all tested levels tell us, and what does the weaker correlation between school variables and achievement at the same levels tell us?

Such correlations are often interpreted in the context of equality of educational opportunity and are cast in terms of "closing the gap" between rich and poor. My third point is that the IEA data provide incomplete information about the effect of schools on the gap between countries or groups within countries. One interpretation of the relatively strong relationship between background and achievement is that schools do not reduce the gap between groups of high and low levels of home background, and thus do not reduce the initial inequality. If we define the equalizing task of schools as scrambling the original rank order of children on achievement, the schools appear to fail. But a different definition of reducing inequality can lead to a different conclusion.

Recall the hypothetical example given above. Although the rank order of home background groups was the same both before school and at fifth grade, schooling was hypothesized to have provided a large absolute core of knowledge to all children. In the situation before schooling, children from the most advantaged home background scored ten times higher than children from the least advantaged, whereas the ratio between the highest and lowest groups in absolute knowledge in the fifth grade was only 1.1 to 1, a dramatic drop from 10 to 1. Unfortunately, of course, we do not have absolute measures of achievement to help us detect whether something like this is happening. Our reliance on normative measures does not allow us to make comparisons of this sort. But data from the IEA and other United States data tell us something about achievement. These data indicate that by the age of about ten almost all children can carry out the basic function of decoding in reading and have some minimal comprehension skills. Other data also indicate that by the same age almost all children can carry out basic arithmetic tasks. Still other data attest to the great body of common knowledge about history, science, and geography that is shared by the majority of this age group. It seems reasonable to conclude that schools play a role in transmitting such knowledge and that without school opportunities to learn would be distributed with much greater inequity.

Thus to conclude that schooling does not close the gap between originally differing groups seems true if we consider the important criterion to be one of relative order. If we conceive of the problem in terms of an absolute measure of achievement which might be influenced by a large common core of school-learned information, the stability of the relationship between home background and achievement across grade levels tells us very little.

The final point comes closer to the issues addressed in Coleman's paper. The issue is whether the IEA data tell us much about the differential impact of variations in school-related inputs. In principle, at least, the IEA might be very informative here. Three points are particularly important, at least with regard to the United States. First, on the measures used in the IEA and in other surveys like the Coleman study of equality of opportunity there are few differences among schools. In most schools, for example, there is a fairly wide range of experienced and inexperienced teachers. And among schools, especially within regions of the country, there is a fairly small range of different class sizes. Also, schools of the United States are remarkably similar in their curriculum, particularly at the elementary level. Over 50 percent of the schools in the nation use one of four practically indistinguishable reading series. Thus on the types of variables that can be measured by a survey questionnaire (always with some error) there may exist too little true variation to enable us confidently to make estimates of effects.

Second, the types of data that can be collected by survey questionnaires suffer from a potentially more important defect: the questionnaire items generally tap discrete characteristics of schools and classrooms without regard for the context in which the elements exist. Without some measures of the context, we have little hope of getting reasonable estimates of the effects of most of the types of school variables assessed in the IEA. Consider, for example, class size as a variable. Assessed across all contexts in a survey, what would we expect the effect of variation in class size to be? In part of the sample the context might include a teacher trying to individualize instruction in reading. In this context, variation in class size might be terribly important. Now imagine that in another part of the sample teachers simply follow the conventional strategy of dividing the class into three or four groups. Here differences in class size might bear little relation to achievement. Overall, then, the average relationship, taken out of context and averaged across contexts, is likely to be small, and small it is. I do not believe that survey methodology is, overall, adequate for specification of contexts such as these. Survey questionnaire data do not allow us to specify the important functional relationships among school resources and student achievement.

The third and final issue on what can be learned from the IEA data on changing schools reflects a bit more optimism. While we cannot say much about school effects, the data might be helpful in indicating variables that may influence achievement and thus are worth experimental manipulation. But it is crucial to note that while the data might give us clues about promising variables, it does not give us an assurance on what the effects of the manipulation might be. As Professor Mosteller noted at the Harvard conference, in order to figure out what the effect is of giving the system a kick you need to kick the system. This requires experimental data, not survey data.

5. Implications of the IEA Findings for the Philosophy of Comprehensive Education

Torsten Husén

In considering the issue of comprehensive versus selective schools we are dealing primarily with a social, political, and economic problem rather than with an educational problem. We lack an international terminology in education, at least one that lends itself to a description of educational structures. To an Englishman, "comprehensive school" means a school offering the major secondary school programs under one roof. To an American, it denotes a secondary high school catering to all children drawn from a certain district and providing all kinds of programs. To a Swede, it signifies the basic, organizationally undifferentiated nine-year school. The term thus refers both to the elementary and secondary stage and is conceived by and large in the same way as was the *école unique* in France or the *Einheitsschule* in Germany in the educational debate after World War I. During the last decade *Gesamtschule* in the latter country has referred to an integrated school covering the entire compulsory school period.

A comprehensive system provides a common, publicly supported education for all children of mandatory school age in a given area. This implies that all programs or curricular offerings are provided within the same school unit. Another essential feature of comprehensiveness is that no differentiation or grouping practices that decisively determine the ensuing educational and vocational careers are employed and that children from all walks of life are taken care of with a minimum of social bias.

All educational institutions are indeed more or less selective in terms of both access and attrition rates, such as the repeating of grades and dropping out.[1] National systems vary tremendously, however, in the severity with which they employ selective practices. In some countries there are almost no restrictions on enrollment during the age range covered by mandatory schooling. The choice of optional programs is up to the pupil and his parents. For instance, the nine-year basic school in Sweden is prohibited by law from selecting students for the various options in grades seven through nine, whereas at the age of sixteen, when transfer occurs to the upper secondary school, competitive selection to the various programs occurs on the basis of grades obtained in the terminal grade of the basic school. In Western European countries, where transfer from the elementary to the academic secondary school (to which access is rather limited) takes place at ages ten to twelve, competitive selection in terms of both scholastic ability and social background (which are intrinsically correlated) can be rather severe. But there is a marked tendency to bring about greater flexibility and to postpone definitive selection by introducing a guidance period (*cycle d'orientation*). This was introduced by the famous de Gaulle decree in 1959.[2] The *Strukturplan* submitted by the *Deutscher Bildungsrat* in 1969 is of interest in this connection; it speaks explicitly of an "orientation phase."[3]

Other types of selectivity also vary greatly. The repeating of grades during compulsory schooling, particularly in the elementary school, is almost nonexistent in some countries. Promotion from one grade to another takes place on the basis of chronological age. In other systems considerable repeating of grades has already taken place in the first grade of the elementary school.[4]

The main forces behind the change from a selective-elitist school structure to a more comprehensive school structure in many European countries can be categorized under three main headings: an improved standard of living, democratization, and mass education.

An improved standard of living and improved public welfare have been conducive to heightened aspirations in terms of self-realization and an increased individual demand for education. This increase is sometimes referred to as "social demand" for education.[5] Sweden is a case in point. In his study of the Swedish school reform Paulston shows that after the establishment and implementation of basic reforms aimed at establishing social welfare and full employment, there were demands for a reform of the structure of the educational system that would increase participation and broaden access.[6]

Democratization, particularly of secondary and higher education, was aimed at equalizing opportunities and opening up educational careers for talented students from lower-class homes. "Equality of opportunity" became in the 1960s one of the catch phrases behind the attempts to reshape the structure of the educational system by removing geographic, economic, and psychological barriers that hinder children from underprivileged homes in getting access to high-level education.[7] The demand for equality, however, does not imply identity in treatment. In its recommendations the *Deutscher Bildungsrat* stated: "The task is rather to equalize the opportunity early and to differentiate the offerings of the educational system later in order to promote the abilities and interests of the young people and to see to it that further education gives the corresponding offering."[8]

The classical liberal conception of "equality of opportunity" has been that geographic and economic barriers should be reduced or entirely removed in order to give all children, irrespective of social background, the same chance to compete in climbing the educational (and social) ladder. As has been pointed out elsewhere, those in the Swedish Labor party who were framing the party's school policy during the 1920s and 1930s were even ready tacitly to accept an elitist educational system, provided support in terms of stipends or removal of tuition fees could be given to lower-class students.[9]

Under the impact of research conducted since the middle 1960s the liberal conception of equality of opportunity has been seriously challenged.[10] Educational equality was previously thought to have its starting point with the inherited ability to absorb school learning. The students had varying "natural capacities" that had been bestowed upon them at birth. Educational policy, therefore, should aim at giving everyone an education that brought him to the optimum of his capacities. Society had only to see to it that material circumstances did not prevent the individual from utilizing his God-given, unchangeable talent by obtaining a suitable education to promote his career. If he had been admitted to a chosen school or program and then failed in it, the responsibility was primarily his, not that of the system.

During the 1960s one became aware of the tremendous, though subtle, influence exerted by the home in providing the child with learning tools, increasing his vocabulary, interacting with him in order to train him to carry out tasks by himself, and influencing his attitudes and motivation. "Ability to learn" is to a large extent acquired at home during the preschool age. The reason why lower-class children fail at school to such a great extent in comparison with middle- or upper-class children is chiefly their lack of certain skills that are basic prerequisites for success in school learning. In France, for instance, repetition of a grade at the early stage of the *école primaire* is much more frequent among children with working-class backgrounds than among the rest.[11]

Thus, the task of the school and of society at large cannot be confined to providing merely a formal equality in material terms by, for instance, giving everyone free access to the same basic education provided in schools with uniform resources and standards. It is also up to these agents to provide every child with the ability he requires in order to profit successfully from the education offered him by the system. The school, therefore, must provide compensatory education for those with environmental handicaps. This necessity applies particularly to institutions catering to children of preschool age. Intellectual differentiation as measured by so-called intelligence tests takes place chiefly before children enter elementary school.[12]

Research conducted since the 1950s has made us aware that selective measures of all kinds, such as repeating of grades and dropping out, are related to social background.[13] According to the traditional philosophy of equality of opportunity everyone should have the same chance to compete on the basis of his "native capacity." One's socioeconomic handicaps have to be compensated for by material support in terms of free places or stipends. But what is meant by "ability"? The criteria used in selecting students could be placed in one of three categories: test scores (on intelligence and/or achievement tests); school marks; and examinations (entrance or final examinations). All these criteria are to varying degrees correlated with variables in social background, such as parental education and other socioeconomic indexes. Thus, selection as such means that there is a tendency, sometimes weak but at other times quite strong, to give precedence to pupils with a more privileged home background. Floud and his co-workers evaluated the effect of the "democratization" of grammar school selection at age eleven-plus in England, as sup- posedly achieved by the 1944 Education Act.[14] They found that when all grammar school places were thrown open to those who did well on the eleven-plus examination the proportion of working-class children decreased, whereas the proportion of middle-class children increased. Previously, when fees had to be paid, a given number of free places were kept open for children from lower-class homes.

The earlier the stage at which selection takes place, the more strongly the social factors operate. The child of ten to twelve could not reasonably be expected to be actively and rationally involved in his future educational and occupational career decisions to the same extent as a youngster of fifteen or sixteen. The IEA mathematics survey showed that where selection for academic secondary educa- tion takes place at an early age the social class structure of the school enrollment differs more markedly from the social composition of the general population than is the case in countries where transfer takes place late or where the system throughout the entire mandatory school age is comprehensive, that is, provides all children in a certain area all kinds of education under the same roof.[15]

Mass education at the upper secondary and at the tertiary levels, referred to as the "educational explosion," has been a reflection of both the rapidly growing need for trained manpower and an increas- ing "educational consumption." These forces, however, conflict with a school organization and a curriculum designed for an economy that is somewhat static and a society with a rigid and elitist social struc- ture.

Until now both the occupational structure and the social stratifi- cation system in most industrialized countries could be depicted by a pyramid, at the bottom of which was a majority consisting of un- skilled or semiskilled manual workers.[16] Most of them had a modest formal education given by a compulsory elementary school that until recently has varied in length from six to eight or nine years. The next level consisted mainly of white-collar workers, such as clerical workers and those in sales, supervisors in industry, and nurses. The formal education required in most cases exceeded elementary school by a few years and was usually some kind of middle school with graduation at fifteen or sixteen with a credential that did not qualify one for entrance to a university. The middle schools were either separate establishments or consisted of the lower section of the preuniversity, academic secondary school. At the top of the pyramid was a small percent of the age group that had been graduated from the academic preuniversity school and the university. Persons with these qualifications made up the professional occupations.

In contrast, the occupational structure in economically highly developed countries that are now on their way into the postindustrial society increasingly takes the shape of an egg. At the bottom of the status hierarchy are a diminishing number of occupations that require only a modest amount of formal schooling followed by on-the-job vocational training. In the middle, one finds an increasing number of occupations requiring formal education extending to the age of sixteen to eighteen and followed by a specialized vocational training. At the top, the number of persons with higher education and professional occupations increases rapidly.

In countries such as the Federal Republic of Germany and England it has been repeatedly emphasized that a reorganization of school structure ought to be based on adequate empirical research. Both adherents of an elitist system and those in favor of an unselective school usually agree that before policy makers decide to "go comprehensive" they should have evidence showing to what extent this means an improvement or an impairment. A problem that is seldom raised explicitly, however, is that different opinions exist regarding the criteria to be chosen as indicators of adequacy or efficiency of the system. Those who favor a parallel, bipartite system tend to measure the quality of the end products of the system, that is, those who survive until graduation or certification; those who favor a unified, comprehensive system tend to consider the quality of education given to all students who enter the system. Evidently the criterion of the end product tends to favor an elitist system, whereas the "all student" criterion is more compatible with a comprehensive philosophy. But even if agreement on employing only one of these two types of general criteria could be reached, there would still be difficulties in reaching a consensus about the specific criteria to be employed in assessing attainments of students. What emphasis should be put on learning "hard facts" as compared to skills? How should factual knowledge be weighed in comparison with the ability to learn new things? How should factual knowledge be weighed in comparison with the ability to learn new things? How important are noncognitive objectives, such as independence, ability to cooperate, and ability to take responsibility? Those who prefer a bipartite system tend to value skills and affective objectives less highly than do those who favor a comprehensive system.

Thus, the issue of the comprehensive versus the selective school provides another illustration of a problem pointed out by Myrdal in the 1930s and recently taken up by him again: the role of implicit values in the social sciences.[17] It would take us too far to spell out the problem here. Suffice it to point out that the social researcher is guided by his own value preferences not only in choosing the problems he sets out to investigate, but also in selecting the variables that he sees as relevant and in interpreting his findings. This does not mean, however, that researchers are dependent upon their different value premises to the extent that they would operate in perfect solipsistic isolation from each other. Such a view would in this case imply that the researcher with a selective bias would consistently end up with facts favoring an elitist system, whereas the comprehensively biased researcher would only produce evidence supporting a comprehensive system. Consensus can be reached by defining carefully certain circumscribed problems that lend themselves to investigations that can be interpreted uniformly and independently of the value premises. For instance, in terms of scores on standardized examinations, in which of the two systems do students on the average score higher? Is it possible in a comprehensive system to bring the elite, say the top 10 percent of the students within an age group, to the same level of competence as in a selective system?

The debate on the relative merits and drawbacks of a comprehensive and selective system of education can be subsumed under five categories of arguments and counterarguments.

First, those favoring a selective system contend that the top students in a comprehensive system will suffer by having to be taught together with their peers who learn more slowly. Mixing will impair the top students' standard of achievement in comparison with students of equal intellectual standing in countries where an organizational differentiation in separate academic schools takes place at an early age or where strict ability grouping within the schools is employed. The comprehensivists, on the other hand, maintain that the top students will not suffer as much as the majority of students in a selective system who remain in the elementary school after the academics have been selected for transfer to the secondary school that prepares them for the university. The less "book-oriented" majority tends to attain less in a selective than in a comprehensive system.

Second, an early differentiation should be made, if for nothing else than purely pedagogical reasons, between those who the school thinks hold academic promise and those who do not. It is extremely difficult, not to say impossible, to teach classes as heterogeneous with regard to ability as those which are the result of an undifferentiated system. The comprehensivists contend that variability can be taken care of by individualized teaching, using individualized selection of media and/or individualized allocation of time.

Third, a system of selection based on fair and equally employed criteria of academic excellence will open careers to those who deserve it by possessing the necessary (mainly inherited) talent. A selective system is beset with social bias. As one moves up the educational ladder, students of lower-class background show a decreasing participation, both in a selective and in a comprehensive system, but the decrease starts earlier and is more marked in the selective system.

Fourth, a selective system takes individual differences into proper account and allocates all the students to tracks and programs according to their aptitudes. A comprehensive system with a late differentiation tries to keep the options open by not being beset by selection screens and barriers that rule out certain options at an early stage of schooling.

Fifth, a comprehensive system means lowering the standards in the secondary school to the detriment of university education. Some kind of definitive selection at the secondary level would have to be made in order to secure students with good academic potential for the university. The standard in terms of the attainments achieved by the elite in the secondary school in a comprehensive system is not inferior to that in a selective one.

The development of the American high school demonstrates what happens when opportunities at the secondary level are broadened. The enrollment increased from about 500,000 in 1900 to about 7,000,000 in 1940. This corresponded to an increase from 10 to 70 percent of the population within the fourteen to seventeen age bracket. The fact that an additional 15 percent of the relevant age group had entered high school every ten years since the turn of the century gave rise to the question as to whether and to what extent the academic ability among high school entrants had deteriorated in proportion to the increased enrollment. As was later the case in Europe, it was taken for granted that high school students represented a fairly select group from the point of view of ability. This assumption was seldom challenged. Counts, who took advantage of survey data from about 1920, is quoted by Finch as saying that "in a very large measure participation in the privilege of a secondary education is contingent on social and economic status."[18]

The heavily increased enrollment created concern among American high school teachers who were no longer dealing with the top 10 or 15 percent in terms of intelligence, but had to cater to the needs of the below average pupils as well.

Finch attempted to collate all the information available from surveys on high school samples from 1916 on, when group-administered intelligence tests began to be used in American schools. The average intelligence quotient for each survey was plotted against time. Contrary to what many expected, a clear trend toward increased intelligence quotients could be observed. In a few cases retests of children in the same school after some years, when enrollment from the relevant age groups had increased, indicated that "increasing high school enrollment [had] been accompanied by a gain rather than by a loss in the average level of ability, as measured by group tests of intelligence."[19]

One of the main reasons why a heavy increase in enrollment has not been accompanied by a decrease in average scholastic ability is that the small fraction that previously stayed in school beyond primary education did not represent such a superior group intellectually as many people, not least teachers, believed. Social selection must have played an important role, which can be assessed from the figures we have on the social composition of the enrollment in countries where secondary schools until recently have been selective. But when Finch conducted his study no data were available that could cast light upon the problem of whether the level of ability (as measured by group tests) was constant over successive generations. Finch himself hypothesized that such a change had taken place in the United States during the first half of the century. He quoted the studies by the American Youth Commission in the 1930s, according to which economic factors more than ability determined who went to high school. In summing up his findings, Finch suggested that

improved elementary school education along with improved conditions outside of school accounts for the fact that heavily increased enrollment was not accompanied by a decline in average
intelligence of the students.

IEA Findings on the Elite in Selective and Comprehensive Systems

Educational folklore has always been full of beliefs about the
relative quality of education in various countries. Under the impact
of Sputnik in the United States at the end of the 1950s eminent
persons, such as Admiral Rickover, began to add to this folklore by
making sweeping statements about the relative merits of American
and European education. Typical of the spell of masochistic self-
criticism of American education was the eagerness to look for
remedies in Europe that would enable the United States to revise its
secondary education, in particular in order to compete successfully
with the Soviet Union and other countries in producing qualified
scientists and engineers.

Most of the naive comparisons between national school systems
that were made under the impact of Sputnik were based upon assumptions that have until recently never been tested empirically.
Criteria of the outcomes of national educational systems have so far
often been figures on enrollment or graduation, but no international
criteria for educational quality, such as internationally valid attainment tests, have been devised.[20] Within countries there is a rather
high degree of uniformity in educational structure and practices,
whereas across countries there are considerable differences. By relating input factors (such as the social background of students, competence of teachers, characteristics of the curriculum, and teaching
practices) to outcomes in terms of achievement and attitudes toward
school learning, more informative cross-national comparisons could
be made. By multinational replications of the same analyses we could
identify factors that decisively influence student achievement. In
order to identify such factors and to carry out meaningful comparisons among countries, we need to establish internationally valid
yardsticks by which to assess the standards of pupils at certain grade
or age levels or at certain terminal points (for instance, at the end of
the preuniversity school).[21]

The term "standard" has a time-honored place in educational

folklore; it often has connotations of self-evidence conducive to the belief that it is metaphysically anchored. The accusation of "lowering standards" is frequently leveled in order to counter attempts at changing the educational structure so as to broaden opportunities. When the elitist type of secondary academic schools in Sweden was gradually replaced during the 1950s and 1960s by comprehensive schools providing universal secondary education, a common objection was that the new system would "lower the standards." The new schools had to disprove the contention that "more means worse" by being subjected to continuous comparisons with the selective secondary schools. For almost a decade it was not recognized that one cannot compare a comprehensive with a selective educational system solely in terms of their respective end products. In the first place, one has also to evaluate the systems in terms of the price paid for the quality of the end products. And what is the attrition rate?[22] Secondly, one has to consider the "productivity" of an educational system by asking "How many are brought how far?" We shall focus here on a third type of question where a fair comparison can be made, namely "Is the standard of the elite lower in a comprehensive than in a selective system?"

In attempting to answer this question we shall draw upon the findings of the IEA multinational surveys in mathematics and science. The IEA studies were not launched primarily to make global comparisons among countries. The cooperating research centers did not intend to conduct a kind of "cognitive Olympics." The overall aim was to relate certain social, economic, and pedagogic characteristics of the different systems to the outcomes of instruction in terms of student achievement and attitudes. Thus, the IEA project was designed to study the relationships within countries between education and salient social and economic factors. An educational system does not operate in a socioeconomic vacuum. The change in school structure from a dual, class-stratified system to a more integrated and unitary one, which we are witnessing in several European countries, reflects a trend toward a society and an economy with a rapidly increasing need for highly trained manpower. Such a need cannot be satisfied by an elitist system based on social and intellectual selectivity.

The IEA mathematics study comprised random samples from four target populations at the thirteen-year-old and preuniversity levels:

all students aged thirteen years to thirteen years, eleven months, on the day of testing; all students at the grade level where the majority of students thirteen years to thirteen years, eleven months, were to be found; all preuniversity students studying mathematics as an integral part of their course for future training or as part of their preuniversity studies; and all preuniversity students studying mathematics as a complementary part of their studies, and the remainder who did not take mathematics at all.[23] The science survey comprised random samples from three large populations: students aged ten years to ten years, eleven months (when they still were taught in all countries by one teacher in a self-contained classroom); students aged fourteen years to fourteen years, eleven months; and students in the grade from which transfer to the university occurs.

Briefly stated, the rationale behind choosing the IEA populations was as follows. If one wants to analyze the relationship between such factors as pupil's age upon entering school, educational and occupational status of parents, competence of teachers, amount of homework, and number of hours of instruction, on the one hand, and the outcomes of instruction, on the other hand, there are reasons for choosing an age when all are still at school to ensure a representative sample of the total age group. In 1964 the age of thirteen proved to be best for this purpose. It was found in 1970 that practically all children at the age of fourteen were in full-time schooling in the industrialized countries. In some countries the grade with the majority of thirteen-year-olds consisted of those left in elementary school after the academic secondary school had siphoned off the "cream." In other countries practically all the thirteen-year-olds were found in the same grade. The preuniversity group lends itself to studies of the retention rate and factors associated with selectivity. Together with an intermediate group of fifteen- to sixteen-year-olds (in the last grade of compulsory schooling) tested in a few countries, the preuniversity group constitutes part of the basis for analyzing the "total yield" of the educational systems under study.[24]

At the end of the 1950s the College Entrance Examination Board sponsored a conference on "talent hunting," a most fitting theme during the period of intensive soul-searching in the United States after the shock of Sputnik. A European scholar in comparative education gave a lecture on "talent hunting abroad," in which he described the high standards achieved by those leaving the upper secondary school in European countries and emphasized the high level of intellectual excellence on which undergraduate university education could be built. In the discussion that followed, I pointed out that what had been so accurately and competently described was the high standard reached by the intellectual and social elite that had survived the various screening procedures in the academic secondary school in Europe. These students consisted at that time of 5 to 10 percent of an age group as compared to over 60 percent in the United States. In order to make a fair comparison, therefore, one should take the top 15 percent of high school graduates in the United States and compare them with the entire "high school graduating group" in European countries.

The second column in Table 5-1 gives the retention figures for 1964, when the data for the IEA mathematics survey were collected.[25] About 70 percent of an age group in the United States and more than 50 percent in Japan were in the final year of the secondary school, as compared to less than 20 percent in most of the European countries that participated in the IEA mathematics study.

But not even a comparison that takes into account the differences among countries with regard to the proportion of the total age group reaching the preuniversity level would be "fair." One should also take into account the price paid for the high standard achieved by the few. In that price one should include the able pupils from low socioeconomic strata who have not been given the chance to realize their potentialities because of the selective structure of the school system. In several European countries, children aged ten to twelve are still divided into two categories: the "academic goats" and the "nonacademic sheep." A dual-track system thus reflects the traditional class stratification of the society. Students at that age do not have articulate plans for their educational and vocational careers. Decisions are made by their parents in terms of social ambitions and economic resources. Furthermore, the attrition rate, resulting from either dropping out or repeating grades, is often very high in the traditional European academic secondary school. The relationship established in the IEA mathematics study between selectivity (or its reverse, "retentivity"), on the one hand, and social background of the preuniversity students, on the other, is given in the third through the sixth columns in Table 5-1. An index of 100 means that a group is fairly represented, whereas more than 100 indicates overrepresentation and less than 100 underrepresentation. As can be seen from

Table 5-1

Relationship between retentivity and social class composition
of enrollment at the preuniversity level

Country	Retentivity indexes				
	(1) Percent of total age group in preuniversity year	(2) Professionals, managers, high technical executives (groups 1 and 2)	(3) Middle-class sub-professionals, clerks, working proprietors, etc. (groups 3, 4, and 6)	(4) Farm proprietors and farm laborers (groups 5 and 8)	(5) Working-class skilled, semiskilled, and unskilled (groups 7 and 9)
United States	70	117	120	129	85
Japan	57	204	114	79	48
Sweden	23	344	169	30	48
Scotland	18	364	200	100	48
Finland	14	272	117	94	58
Belgium	13	263	126	110	51
England	12	620	134	75	31
France	11	538	161	119	-
Federal Republic of Germany	11	589	113	45	12

Source: International Study of Achievement in Mathematics: Phase I, A Comparison of Twelve Countries, ed. Torsten Husén *et al.* (New York: John Wiley; Stockholm: Almqvist & Wiksell, 1967), II, 113.

Table 5-1, the higher the retentivity the lower the social bias. In the Federal Republic of Germany, for example, which both in 1964 and in 1970 had a rather low retentivity, students whose parents are professionals, managers, and executives are vastly overrepresented, whereas working-class students are strongly underrepresented.

Let us now compare countries as to the mean achievement at the preuniversity level and begin with students for whom mathematics is a primary subject. As can be seen from the dotted line in Figure 5-1, the average mathematics score among United States high school graduates taking mathematics is far below that of all other countries. We should take into account, however, that in the United States about 18 percent of the group aged seventeen and eighteen took mathematics and science in the graduating class as compared to only

Mean Mathematics Score

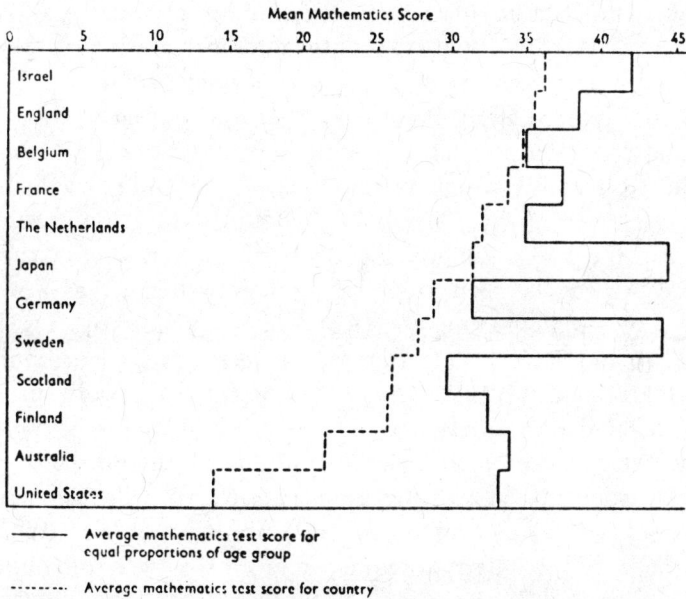

Figure 5-1
Mean mathematics test scores for the total sample and for equal
proportions of age group in each country for terminal mathematics
populations (from *International Study of Achievement in
Mathematics,* ed. Husén *et al.*, II, 124)

4 to 5 percent of the age group in England or the Federal Republic
of Germany. The problem could thus be more fruitfully restated: To
what extent has it been possible within a comprehensive system like
that in the United States to produce an elite comparable in size and
quality to the one produced within a European selective system? One
way of answering this question is to compare equal proportions of
the age groups in the respective countries. The dotted line in Figure
5-1 gives the average performance of all terminal mathematics pupils
in the twelve countries. But when we compare the average score of
the top 4 percent of the corresponding age group, a proportion
selected because it represents the lowest relative number of students
in any country taking mathematics, we obtain the results represented
by the solid line. The range among countries is then much narrower
than for the entire group of terminal mathematics students. The top

4 percent of US students score at about the same level as those in other countries. Two countries with a comprehensive system up to the age of fifteen or sixteen, Japan and Sweden, score the highest of all. On the basis of the distribution of scores among all the terminal mathematics students in all the countries, international standards can be obtained in terms of percentile scores. Figure 5-2 gives the percent of the total age group within each country that has reached the standard achieved by the upper tenth of all the terminal mathematics students. As can be seen, none of the comprehensive and/or highly retentive systems is among the five countries at the bottom, whereas two, Japan and Sweden, together with England, are found at the top.

The mathematics investigations thus revealed a sharply fluctuating average level in the various countries among students in the senior, preuniversity class. These comparisons of overall means were not, however, especially interesting unless allowance was also made for variations between the retention rates of the countries. When that was done, and equal proportions of groups were compared, there were considerably fewer variations on an average. The elites in most countries proved to lie, by and large, on the same level.

Does the same relationship govern in science? We decided to compare first the best 9 percent of the tested population within the industrial countries. This percent was chosen because it was the lowest proportion of the age group in any of the countries representing graduates from the upper secondary school.[26] To arrive at measures of two smaller elite groups we also chose 5 percent and 1 percent, respectively. In Table 5-1 the means for the graduates in participating industrial countries are indicated for the whole sample, for the best 9 percent, for the best 5 percent, and for the best 1 percent of the corresponding age group. The retention rate, that is, the proportion of the population of the relevant age group that is actually in school, is given in the second column in Table 5-2.

As will be seen from Table 5-2 and Figure 5-3, the means for the entire population range from 30.8 for New Zealand to 14.2 for the United States. The former country has a retention rate of thirteen, and the latter has a retention rate of seventy-five. Sweden, with a retention rate of forty-five, shows a mean score of 20.1 for all students tested. Hungary, with a retention rate of twenty-eight, has a mean score of 20.4, whereas Australia, with a retention rate of twenty-nine, shows a mean score of 26.1. If we then compare the

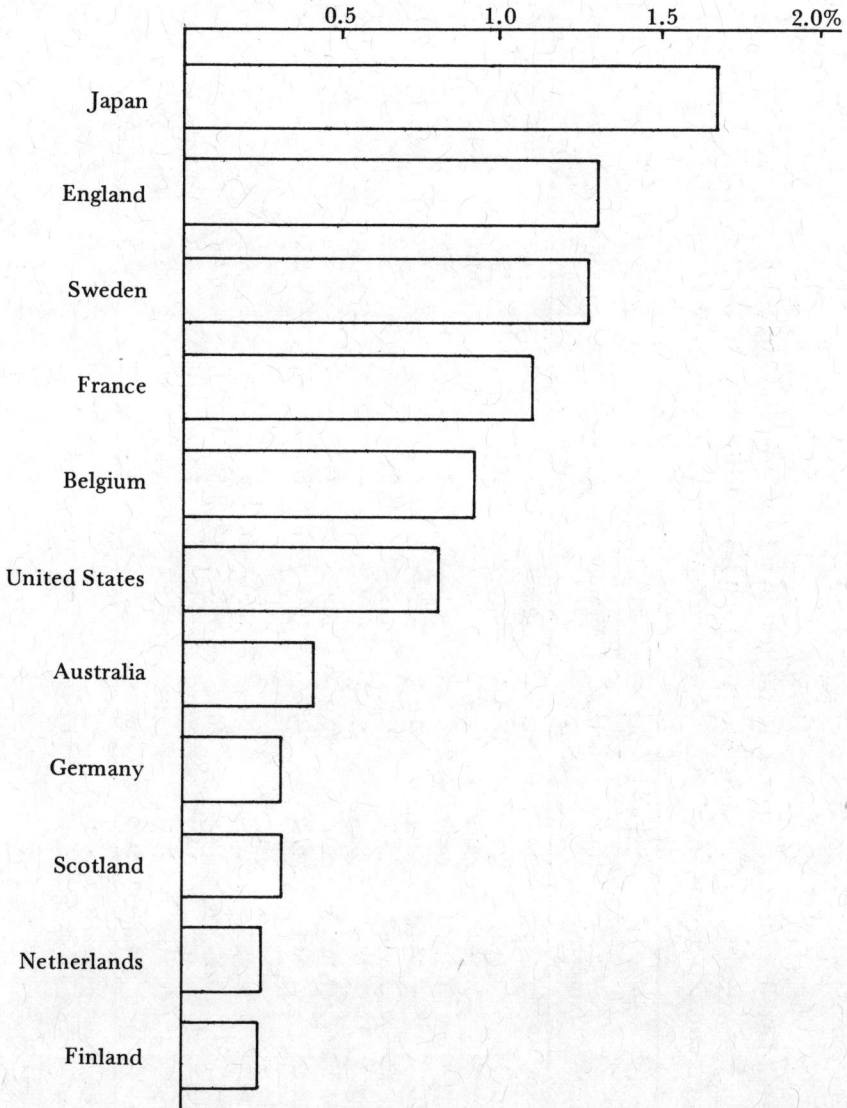

Figure 5-2
Percent of age group reaching upper tenth of terminal mathematics
pupils by international standards (based on data reported in
International Study of Achievement in Mathematics,
ed. Husén *et al.*, II, 131, Table 3.41)

Table 5-2

Means and standard deviations of scores on the test in science for all the graduates from the upper-secondary (preuniversity) school and for the best 9 percent, 5 percent, and 1 percent of the entire corresponding age group

Country	Percent at school[a]	Number of students	Full sample		Top 1 percent		Top 5 percent		Top 9 percent	
			Mean	Standard deviation	Mean	Standard deviation	Mean	Standard deviation	Mean	Standard deviation
New Zealand	13	1,676	30.8	12.6	52.8	2.8	43.5	5.9	36.8	9.0
England	20	2,181	24.4	12.4	51.6	3.2	41.6	6.5	35.5	8.5
Australia	29	4,194	26.1	11.5	51.5	3.2	44.0	4.7	39.9	5.9
Scotland	17	1,321	24.4	12.9	50.7	3.8	40.6	6.4	34.4	8.7
Sweden	45	2,754	20.1	10.9	49.5	3.4	41.2	5.3	37.0	6.2
Hungary	28	2,828	24.0	9.6	48.0	3.8	39.0	5.4	35.0	6.1
Netherlands	13	1,138	24.4	12.0	47.1	3.6	37.2	6.5	30.3	9.4
Finland	21	1,725	20.8	10.5	46.0	4.1	35.7	6.4	30.7	7.4
United States	75	2,514	14.2	9.9	45.8	2.8	36.8	5.5	33.1	5.9
Federal Republic of Germany	9	1,989	28.4	9.6	45.0	4.1	35.3	6.2	28.4	9.6
France	29	3,523	19.1	9.1	40.5	3.5	33.3	4.4	29.9	5.1
Belgium (Flemish)	47	467	18.1	8.5	39.8	3.7	33.0	4.0	30.5	4.2
Italy	16	15,719	16.5	9.2	38.2	4.7	27.4	6.5	22.7	7.3
Belgium (French)	47	941	16.0	8.3	36.2	2.0	30.9	3.1	28.4	3.7

[a]Proportion of the whole age group that attends school.

Source: Comber and Keeves, Science Education in Nineteen Countries, 174.

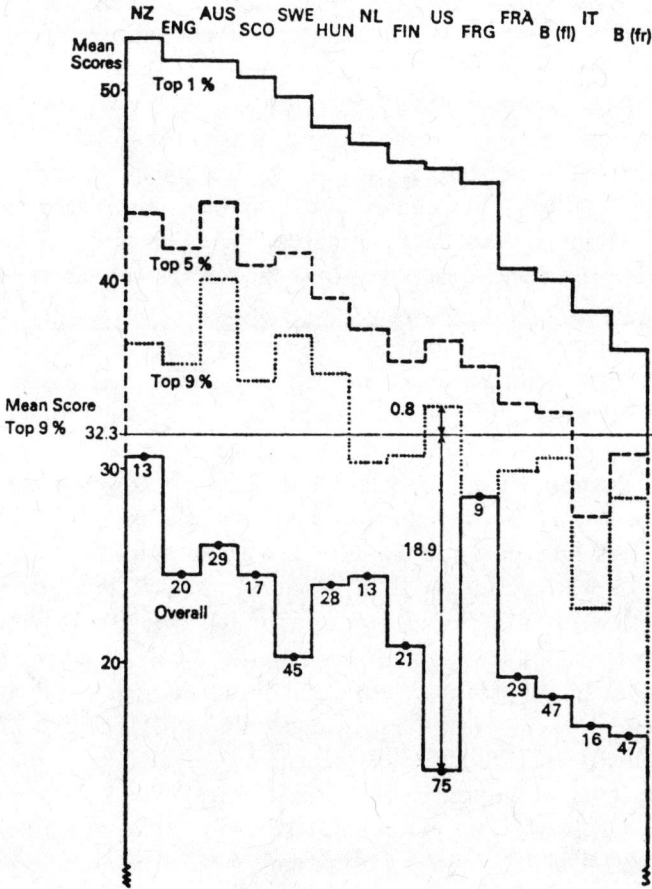

Figure 5-3
Mean scores of top 1 percent, top 5 percent, top 9 percent, and
overall group (from Comber and Keeves,
Science Education in Nineteen Countries, 175)

means for the top 9 percent of the population we find that means for
countries with a broad recruitment base (that is, high retention rates)
increase sharply. The mean score of this group is highest for Australia
with Sweden the next highest. The mean score of this group in the
United States is more than double the mean score for that country
for all students tested and is higher than the comparable scores for
West Germany and France. If we next examine the means for the top

5 percent of students tested in each country we find that countries with a broad recruitment base move ahead even more. For the top 1 percent of students tested in each country the highest means were achieved in four Commonwealth countries with fairly similar educational systems: New Zealand, England, Australia, and Scotland. Next comes Sweden, somewhat ahead of other European countries.

Another method of evaluating a national system of education is to employ certain international standards. This gives more information than mean scores with respect to how far the system carries the great mass of young people forward to certain levels of competence. The analyses reported below build upon the mean for the total score on the science test, including certain items termed "advanced general science." International percentiles (for the industrial countries) were calculated for the 95, 90, 85, 75, and 25 percent levels. We are thus able to determine how many students in each country exceed the international standard for the top 5 percent, the top 10 percent, and so on. It will be seen from Table 5-3, for example, that the average score of 43.3 at the ninety-fifth percentile is exceeded by 3 percent of preuniversity students in Sweden, or by 2 percent of the whole age group.

As was observed in the international report on science,[27] the comparisons made here must take into account the fact that countries vary somewhat in their definitions of the target population for the particular level under study. The definition called for the sampling of those students who were qualified to enter universities and other institutions of higher learning upon completion of secondary school. Since the entrance requirements in Sweden were changed at the time this investigation was completed to include ad hoc entry for students in continuation school (the *fackskole*, a two-year semivocational school at the upper secondary level), it was decided to make provision for them in spite of their limited qualifications. In West Germany, on the other hand, the study was limited to those pupils who after grade thirteen found themselves in the senior *Gymnasium* class (*Oberprima*).

In Table 5-3 we have compared the countries with respect to the proportions of the sample that attain certain international standards. If we start with the ninety-fifth percentile (that is, with the 5 percent at the top) we find that New Zealand is distinctly superior to the other countries. This superiority also holds for other percentiles, the

Table 5-3

Proportion of students in the preuniversity grade and
corresponding proportions estimated for the whole age group
that attains certain international percentile norms on the test in science

Students, by country	Holding power or retentivity	International percentiles and scores					
		25th	50th	75th	85th	90th	95th
		13.1	20.6	29.5	34.8	38.7	43.3
Preuniversity grade							
Australia	29	87	64	38	24	16	8
Belgium (Flemish)	47	70	39	10	2	1	1
Belgium (French)	47	60	28	6	1	0	0
England	20	82	57	31	21	16	9
Federal Republic of Germany	9	95	78	45	26	16	6
Finland	21	74	45	20	11	7	3
France	29	72	41	14	5	2	1
Hungary	28	87	62	27	14	8	4
Italy	16	59	29	9	4	3	1
Netherlands	13	79	56	34	23	16	7
New Zealand	13	91	77	56	42	33	21
Scotland	17	78	56	35	23	17	9
Sweden	45	71	42	20	11	7	3
United States	75	48	24	8	4	2	1
RANGE	66	47	54	48	41	33	21
Whole age group							
Australia	29	25	19	11	7	5	2
Belgium (Flemish)	47	33	18	5	1	1	0
Belgium (French)	47	28	13	3	1	0	0
England	20	16	11	6	4	3	2
Federal Republic of Germany	9	9	7	4	2	1	1
Finland	21	15	9	4	2	1	1
France	29	21	12	4	1	1	0
Hungary	28	24	17	7	4	2	1
Italy	16	9	5	1	1	0	0
Netherlands	13	10	7	4	3	2	1
New Zealand	13	12	10	7	5	4	3
Scotland	17	13	9	6	4	3	2
Sweden	45	32	19	9	5	3	2
United States	75	36	18	6	3	2	1
RANGE	66	27	14	10	6	5	3

Source: Comber and Keeves, *Science Education in Nineteen Countries*, 180.

top 10 percent and so on, a finding that could be expected in view of the high average performance of the preuniversity students of that country. England, Scotland, and Australia also have high proportions of students above the international 5 percent standard.

The question of what a school system produces with its students is pertinent, however, not only to how far it carries those who remain at the level under study, but also to what happens to those who have left the system for various reasons. It would be helpful to know about the formal educational experience (or, in the majority of cases, the lack of such experience) of those who have not "stuck it out" to the end of preuniversity school. In other words, what about the educational standard of the whole age group at this level? Since we obviously were in no position to administer achievement tests to those who no longer attended school, we were compelled to make a reasonable assumption about the level below which the vast majority of those who have left the system may be thought to lie. (See the lower portion of Table 5-3.) In countries where the majority leave school at the age of fourteen or fifteen, and thus by the time they are eighteen or nineteen have been out of school for several years, it does not appear unreasonable to expect those who have left school to fall below the twenty-fifth percentile of those who graduate from upper secondary school. This standard roughly equates with the value attained by the average of high school seniors in the United States. In other countries, such as Sweden, where a great many students have left at the age of sixteen, it may be dubious whether the assumption holds. We have applied it, however, throughout the whole series of countries.

I shall discuss Sweden here because its change to a comprehensive system with a spectacular broadening of the enrollment to the upper secondary school has been seen by critics as an act of "lowering the standards."

If we determine how large a part of the whole age group lies above the ninety-fifth percentile, we find that Sweden with its 2 percent joins the company of the four Commonwealth countries at the top. By taking all factors into consideration, we find that those countries which have a broad recruitment base and/or have recently broadened it also show a high standard. But Sweden also stands relatively high when it comes to the twenty-fifth and fiftieth percentiles. This means that below average students in a system with a broad recruitment base may very well achieve respectable results by international standards.

In summary, the following can be stated. According to the criteria of elitism devised here (that is, the standard specified as a mean for equally large proportions of the age group), students in the Swedish upper secondary school clearly lie above the international average in science. Regarding the second criterion—what the school system produces with the vast majority of its students—the following points may be noted. The Swedish mean works out a bit below the international average. Here it should be remembered that the Swedish sample embraces both the continuation school and the *Gymnasium* (the regular preuniversity school), whereas the other European countries with more narrowly defined qualifications for university entrance have limited themselves to *Gymnasium* students. When the proportion of the age group in school is appropriately allowed for, we find that the Swedish average, like the American one, is strongly influenced by the breadth of recruitment to the indicated level. Analysis of the effect of this broader recruitment base discloses that the Swedish school system ends up on the plus side of the standards ledger. International percentiles have been calculated, making it possible to determine how many within the sampled population, as well as within the whole age group, belong to the top 5, 10, 15, 25, 50, and 75 percent by international standards. We then find that countries with broad recruitment tend, where the whole age group is concerned, to be superior to those with relatively selective systems.

The most reasonable explanation for these findings is that the comprehensive or retentive system provides a broader range of opportunities and a better utilization and development of talent. Systems with an early selection to academic secondary education show a stronger bias in favor of upper- and middle-class students at the preuniversity level than do systems that are more comprehensive or retentive, as well as more flexible in the sense that the final choice between a preuniversity and a vocational program is made between the ages of fifteen and seventeen instead of between the ages of ten and twelve.

As was emphasized earlier, the productivity of a school system ought not to be assessed solely on the basis of the quality of its final products (the students who qualify for university entrance) because we are then comparing widely varying proportions of age groups, and we leave out those who are either excluded from secondary education or do not survive it. We are therefore entitled to put the question thus: How many are brought how far?

The IEA findings suggest that an elite comparable in quality to that of an elite system can be cultivated within a retentive and comprehensive system. In the selective system, however, the high standard of the elite is often bought at the price of low accomplishments by the mass. Selection for the preuniversity school takes place at an early age, and the majority of students are left to complete either an elementary school or a low-prestige program within the secondary school with virtually no chance to transfer to a university preparatory program. In order to be able to assess the total yield we ought to measure the performances of pupils at the intermediate terminal point, when compulsory schooling has been completed. Postlethwaite has used IEA data to show that a higher retention rate is associated with higher "yield," that is, the majority of students in a retentive system tend to achieve better than the corresponding groups in a selective system.[28]

Conclusion

When the Swedish School Commission of 1946 submitted its main report to the government in 1948 and suggested a nine-year comprehensive school to replace all other types of schools covering the period of compulsory education, its recommendations were allegedly based upon commissioned studies on the intellectual development of ability in schoolchildren.[29] Everyone who took part in the debate, pro or con, was at that time convinced that scholastic aptitude was mainly inherited and that the ability to profit from academic programs could be assessed at ages eleven or twelve. But the commission rejected selection for the academic, grammar school type of program at that early age chiefly because this would "deprive" the other programs and the ensuing vocational sectors of their "proper share" of talent. Furthermore, the aptitudes for many of the more "practical" occupations seemed to "mature" later than those for theoretical pursuits. It is unfortunate that both those who were in favor of late differentiation and those against it confused diagnosis with prognosis. It is one thing to measure the actual ability (such as verbal proficiency) of the child, which certainly can be done rather accurately; it is quite another thing to use the score as a predictive index. Effective measures of home environment (including "process variables" covering child-parent interaction) predict success in the secondary academic school better than measures of intelligence and similar indexes.[30] But so far no one has suggested (or has dared to suggest) that social background should be used when selecting children for the grammar school.

The main pedagogical issue, as can be seen from the two "Black Papers"[31] prepared by a group of those against comprehensive education in England, is to what extent the comprehensive system is "lowering standards." In order to come to grips with this problem, one must, of course, define "standard." Though there is much to be said for defining it by the formula of how many are brought how far, a comparative evaluation of comprehensive and selective systems would be incomplete if limited to the end products of the systems, mainly because the price paid for the quality of the end products is not taken into consideration. There is, for example, no point in comparing the average performance of high school graduates in the United States or Japan with those who sit for the *baccalauréat* in France because the former consist of the majority of the corresponding age group, whereas the latter are a clear minority.

The issue of whether a school system (local or national) should "go comprehensive," that is, become integrated or not in terms of social recruitment and programs, cannot, as I have tried to show above, be settled solely on the basis of purely pedagogical considerations. Nor can it be settled by drawing mainly upon evidence from psychological research. The educational system does not, and should not, operate in a social vacuum; it is today more than ever an integral part of the socioeconomic fabric.

Notes

1. Torsten Husén, *Social Background and Educational Career* (Paris: Organization for Economic Cooperation and Development, 1972); *id., Availability and Utilization of Talent* (Amsterdam: Nijhoff, in press).

2. *Reviews of National Policies for Education: France* (Paris: Organization for Economic Cooperation and Development, 1971).

3. Deutscher Bildungsrat, *Empfehlungen der Bildungskommission: Strukturplan für das Bildungswesen* (Bonn: Deutscher Bildungsrat, 1970).

4. *Reviews of National Policies for Education: France* (Paris: Organization for Economic Cooperation and Development, 1970), 56 ff.

5. Organization for Economic Cooperation and Development, Study Group in the Economics of Education, *Social Objectives in Educational Planning* (Paris: Organization for Economic Cooperation and Development, 1967).

6. Ronald Paulston, *Swedish Comprehensive School Reform, 1918-1950: The Period of Formulation and Adoption* (New York: Teachers College Press, Columbia University, 1968).

7. See, for example, *Reviews of National Policies for Education: Germany* (Paris: Organization for Economic Cooperation and Development, 1973).

8. Deutscher Bildungsrat, *op. cit.*, 30.

9. Torsten Husén, "Responsiveness and Resistance in the Educational System to Changing Needs of Society: Some Swedish Experiences," *International Review of Education* 15 (1969): 476-87; see also *id., Social Background and Educational Career.*

10. James S. Coleman, "The Concept of Equality of Educational Opportunity," *Harvard Educational Review* 38 (Winter 1968): 7-37; R. Breton, "Academic Stratification in Secondary Schools and the Educational Plans of Students," *Review of Canadian Sociology and Anthropology Association* 7 (1970): 17-34; Husén, *Availability and Utilization of Talent*, Chapter 6.

11. *Educational Policy and Planning: France* (Paris: Organization for Economic Cooperation and Development, 1972), 105 ff.; see also Alfred Sauvy and Alain Girard, "Les diverses classes sociales devant l'enseignement," *Population* 20 (March-April 1965): 205-32.

12. Benjamin S. Bloom, *Stability and Change in Human Characteristics* (New York: John Wiley, 1964); Benjamin S. Bloom *et al., Compensatory Education for Cultural Deprivation* (New York: Holt, 1964).

13. For a review of the relevant literature, see Husén, *Social Background and Educational Career.*

14. Jean E. Floud (ed.), A. H. Halsey, and F. M. Martin, *Social Class and Educational Opportunity* (London: Heinemann, 1957).

15. *International Study of Achievement in Mathematics: A Comparison of Twelve Countries*, Vols. I and II, ed. Torsten Husén *et al.* (Stockholm: Almqvist & Wiksell, 1967); see also L. C. Comber and John P. Keeves, *Science Education in Nineteen Countries: An Empirical Study*, International Studies in Evaluation, Vol. I (New York: John Wiley; Stockholm: Almqvist & Wiksell, 1973).

16. Torsten Husén, "Lifelong Learning in the 'Educative Society,'" *International Review of Applied Psychology* 17 (1968): 87-99.

17. Gunnar Myrdal, *Objectivity in Social Research* (New York: Pantheon, 1969).

18. F. H. Finch, *Enrollment Increase and the Changes in the Mental Level*, Applied Psychology Monographs, No. 10 (Chicago: University of Chicago Press, 1946), 11.

19. *Ibid.*, 39.

20. See Frederick Harbison and Charles Myers, *Education, Manpower and Economic Growth* (New York: McGraw-Hill, 1964); see also Frederick Harbison, *Human Resources as the Wealth of Nations* (New York: Oxford University Press, 1973), 57 ff.

21. Torsten Husén, "International Impact of Evaluation," in *Educational Evaluation: New Roles, New Means*, Sixty-eighth Yearbook of the National Society for the Study of Education, Part II (Chicago: University of Chicago Press, 1969), 335-50.

22. *Id.*, "Loss of Talent in Selective School Systems," *Comparative Education Review* 4 (October 1960): 70-74.

23. *International Study of Achievement in Mathematics*, ed. Husén *et al.*

24. T. Neville Postlethwaite, *School Organization and School Achievement* (New York: John Wiley, 1967).

25. *International Study of Achievement in Mathematics*, ed. Husén *et al.*

26. Comber and Keeves, *op. cit.*

27. *Ibid.*

28. Postlethwaite, *op. cit.*

29. Torsten Husén, *Problems of Differentiation in Swedish Compulsory Schooling* (Stockholm: Scandinavian University Books, 1962).

30. *Id.*, *Social Background and Educational Career.*

31. C. B. Cox and A. E. Dyson, *Black Paper Two: The Crisis in Education* (London: The Critical Quarterly Society, 1969).

Commentary I

J. R. Gass

Torsten Husén has done it again—plunged into a complicated debate with some good operational questions and a mass of data and emerged with a clear conclusion. "The IEA findings suggest," he says, "that an elite comparable in quality to that of an elite system can be cultivated within a retentive and comprehensive system. In the selective systems, however, the high standard of the elite is often bought at the price of low accomplishments by the mass." Thus, to state the conclusion succinctly, comprehensiveness beats selectivity on its own grounds: educational output.

Since we are discussing the implications of the IEA findings for the philosophy of comprehensive education, let me say first that the debate must be a broader one than implied by the above findings. It was good to insist, as Husén did, that consensus between social scientists "can be reached by defining carefully certain circumscribed

problems that lend themselves to investigations that can be interpreted uniformly and independently of the value premises." This is,
of course, true, but then the findings have to be related to the real
issues that underpin the debate: has the vast growth of education
paid off in human, social, and economic terms, and can we today
reinterpret the "comprehensive" philosophy so as to overcome the
loss of confidence in education as one of the keys to growth,
equality, and human happiness?

Let us note first of all that—unless historians can show otherwise
—affluence as we understand it today, based on technology and
economic rationalization, implies some sort of a social, income, and
occupational hierarchy. The hierarchy could, if we were true
egalitarians, be considered as one of the costs of growth that we
would seek to minimize. The broad lesson from the IEA study is that
the comprehensive system is as good as the selective system in developing elites for the hierarchy, and it is superior in providing the vast
range of middle-level skills needed for the middle of Husén's "egg." I
do not want to fall into the trap of a multifactorial analysis of social
status, educational background, educational performance, occupation, and income, but I wonder if Professor Husén would agree that
the IEA findings are consistent with the following picture. Even
under comprehensive structures, education is largely functioning as a
means of allocating individuals to the occupational and social structure. The social bias in this process is reduced in a comprehensive
system, but remains very powerful. This is partly a consequence of a
failure to solve the pedagogical problems involved when society
brings a high percent of children of each age group into the secondary school and the university, but is more a consequence of the
relative inability of education to override the influences of family
and social class on aspiration and educational performance during
childhood and early youth when children are in school.

If the above is true, my point of departure would be that there
may be diminishing returns from further extensions of comprehensive secondary education for countries at the forefront of educational growth. If, finally, education is allocating individuals to the
social hierarchy in a socially biased fashion, I would like to see more
resources going into opportunities to rethrow the educational dice in
later years, by way of educational opportunities for young, and not
so young, adults. I am suggesting, in simple terms, a civilian version

of the GI Bill of Rights. The social class-education-occupa-
tion-income lockstep should be broken by redistributing educational
opportunities over the life cycle.

If this could become a firm policy, perhaps we could take the risks
of diluting the comprehensive approach at the ages of sixteen to
nineteen, since selection at this age would not be final. Whether we
like it or not the steam is running out of further extensions of
comprehensive secondary education up to, say, eighteen. The reality
that educational equality does not mean giving all the same is taking
root. Would not the IEA agree that we need a variety of learning
environments for young people in this age group on pedagogical as
well as social grounds? I recognize, of course, that the elitists will
agree with me on the point, but surely they defend a differentiated
structure of upper secondary institutions on the assumption that
they are protecting the access of privileged social groups to the
"quality" schools, which lead, in turn, to elite universities and
prestigious professions. Why not give young people access to a wider
range of quality learning environments combined with a right to
return to full- or part-time education as an adult, on the theory that
this is more likely to overcome social disadvantage than a uniform
lockstep pattern of schooling? This would bring the differential
maturation, motivation, and learning patterns of adolescents into the
center of the picture, as opposed to their somewhat marginal place in
Husén's analysis.

It is paradoxical that a move in the direction described above
would reinforce the comprehensive principle at the previous steps of
education, since it would place a premium on bringing as many
youngsters as possible up to, say, age sixteen on equal terms. The
arguments for a comprehensive system up to this age, in the sense of
both access and curricula as defined by Husén, seem to me to be
self-evident unless one is prepared to defend crude educational
privilege. But even here the comprehensive principle must be translated into something that is pedagogically viable. Bloom's "mastery"
principle contains the essential truth that equality does not mean the
same—that with more resources and different school organization the
less able children can "achieve" according to unexpectedly high
levels. This principle seems to me to contain two elements essential
to the future of the comprehensive school up to age sixteen: positive
discrimination in terms of resources; and individualization in terms
of structure, curricula, and pedagogy.

In conclusion, there is in Husén's paper a stubborn faith in the equalizing role of education, which I tend to share. The main thrust of the concept of recurrent education that I have mentioned above is that only if educational opportunities are redistributed over the life cycle will education continue to be central to the debate on equality. If Lucky Jim wins or loses according to the way the dice fall, then let him throw again when he has learned the rules of the game.

Commentary II

Martin Trow

Educational research has various functions: occasionally it tells us things we did not know before, but more often it serves to concentrate the mind and to give us fresh perspectives on perennial questions. I believe that the IEA findings do not really speak to the issues of comprehensive schooling, but Husén's essay does, and the research context helps us to think about the problems he addresses.

Husén first reminds us that "comprehensiveness" of schooling is variable in practice and means different things in different countries. His own conception of comprehensive education involves integration with respect both to enrollment and curricula. "To be genuinely comprehensive the enrollment has to reflect in a representative way the social composition of the community outside the school." But surely it can only be "genuine" in this sense where the school is unchallenged by alternative systems, and especially by parallel selective schools, whether public or private. In Britain, as in many other countries, comprehensive schools exist alongside selective schools and are likely to continue to do so, despite the official doctrine of the Labour party on this question. Comprehensive schools may be more representative of "the broader community" than the selective schools, but in many places, including parts of the United States, they reflect the creaming, both social and academic, by more selective schools. Husén reminds us that "comprehensiveness" is a variable and not an attribute of national educational systems. We might take that reminder seriously, and in our comparisons among countries we should keep in mind the degree to which the system as a whole has gone comprehensive, almost completely, as in Sweden; only partly, as in Britain; or almost not at all, as in West Germany. A comprehensive school in a mixed system is not at all the same as one in a fully comprehensive system: it has been creamed; it is second class in status; and it almost surely does not have first call on the best and most highly qualified teachers.

Now this kind of qualitative data (that is, on the degree to which a system is comprehensive) is, for the most part, missing from the IEA studies. But since Husén wishes to make some comparisons between more or less selective systems, he uses, as an indicator of comprehensiveness, the retentivity of a system, that is, the proportion of the whole age group still in school at a given age. At one point, for example, he summarizes an interesting analysis by noting that an elite comparable in quality to that of an elite system can be cultivated within a retentive and comprehensive system." And throughout his chapter he takes retentivity as a fair indicator of comprehensiveness. (That is also done elsewhere in this volume as, for example, in Chapter 2.)

Now in a historical sense that is probably right. In his brief review of the social forces underlying the change from a selective-elitist to a more comprehensive school structure, Husén shows that the forces of a rising standard of living, growing educational demand, democratization, the change in the concept of equality of educational opportunity, and changes in the occupational structure and in the system of higher education all tend to push systems both toward growth (in part through longer retention of students in formal education) and toward more comprehensive schools or a larger comprehensive sector. But I am not sure that all the forces in modern societies lie in that direction or that the growth of mass and universal secondary education must be accomplished through a wholly comprehensive system. In other words, the trend toward retention and the comprehensive principle are to some extent independent movements. Indeed, when Britain raised the age at which students could leave school to sixteen in 1973, it improved its retentivity without making its system any more comprehensive.

Other forces besides an increased age for leaving school will, of course, "improve" a country's retentivity scores. And I agree with

Husén, for largely the reasons he gives, that the trend will continue to be a steady rise in the proportions remaining longer in secondary schools, at least in Western Europe. The United States, however, is near the saturation point with respect to the secondary school age groups. The question for policy makers will be whether that growth should be carried on in wholly comprehensive systems, as in Sweden, in largely comprehensive systems, as in the United States or Japan, or in mixed systems, as in Britain and most other European nations. Growth is compatible with all these arrangements. And while the strong tides of democratization and egalitarianism are, indeed, forces tending toward the fully comprehensive system, changes in the occupational structure and the growth of mass higher education, while tending to produce longer retentivity in secondary school, are not necessarily at odds with the survival of selective schools. (The strongest forces behind selective schools are their graduates and the parents of selective school students, past, present, and future. In many countries these are passionate and influential groups.)

I believe, and Husén's analysis supports the view, that the slogan "more means worse" is wrong, at least with respect to the ability of systems of high retention to bring their ablest students up to the levels of achievement of the small group of survivors of highly selective systems. I suspect, however, that this result could also be accomplished by systems of high retention that are not wholly comprehensive. But that raises the question of whether it makes a difference if a system is wholly comprehensive or grows alongside a surviving elite sector. I think it does make a difference, if not for achievement (and that is, for me, still an open question), then for the role of the schools in the economic and political life of the society, for their relation to the stratification system, and, in a larger sense, for their role in the national culture.

And here, with one qualification, I agree with Husén's final observation that the educational system does not, and should not, operate in a social vacuum. As he put it, the educational system is today, more than ever, "an integral part of the socioeconomic fabric." And he goes on to say that "therefore, an educational system cannot be shaped chiefly on the basis of pedagogical considerations." Surely the notion of a mixed system with selective schools, both public and private, thriving alongside a growing (if permanently creamed) comprehensive sector, is fundamentally different from the idea of a wholly comprehensive state system. And these different conceptions of education are rooted in different class interests as much as in different philosophical and political traditions.

But, if that is so, what relevance *do* pedagogical considerations have for educational planning? What relevance does research such as the IEA studies have to what Husén sees as fundamentally political decisions? They surely have some influence. Husén himself observes, though without mentioning his own considerable role in that movement,[1] that the research of educational psychologists and sociologists of the 1950s and 1960s undermined the concept of a limited pool of ability, and a bit later it helped to transform the dominant conception of equality of educational opportunity from its liberal form—the removal of individuals' social and economic handicaps—into a more radical form, which places on the schools the responsibility of equalizing group rates of achievement and of creating intelligence instead of just providing opportunities for it to reveal itself.[2]

This body of research then did have important political functions. Among others, it changed the ways in which educational questions were asked and challenged the system of unquestioned assumptions that underpinned traditional educational structures and practices. That research helped to arm political and social forces that were independent of the research itself; it provided, for these forces, powerful arguments and rationales.

But the moment we raise questions concerning the influence of research on educational policy we go beyond the IEA data to characteristics of societies, their populations, and their educational systems and somehow are not captured in IEA measures or regression equations. And that suggests that the measured assessment of educational achievements, and of other characteristics of schools and students undertaken by the IEA studies, can be a significant contribution both to knowledge and to policy only if it is linked to other more qualitative assessments of social structure and educational systems. To forge that link, we shall have to combine the detailed IEA measurements with data on the historical development of school systems, on the characteristics of social groups and categories, on organizational patterns, cultural and religious traditions, and the like. But that may require a somewhat different treatment of the quantitative data themselves. There are some kinds of statistical treatments, and I believe that regression analysis is one of them, that preclude or inhibit the introduction of historical or ethnographic ideas or evidence and create a self-contained universe of variables and coefficients and explained variance. My own feeling is that we must find ways of analyzing these kinds of data that open them to additional insights gained from other ways of learning and knowing, and not least from our own experience. That I find very difficult to do with the data in the form in which they are largely reported and analyzed in the IEA documents. This is no criticism of Husén, whose paper presents and discusses data from this study in ways that do allow us to raise questions about their broader meaning and implications for public policy.

Educational policies, while sometimes made at the national level, are wise when they take into account the special characteristics of regions, class, ethnic groups, and the like. The chairman of the State Planning Committee on Public Education in a European country has spoken to me of the special problems of peasant children in his country's backward provinces—educational problems very different from those posed by the children of workers in his country's industrial areas or of white-collar employees in the capital. Every country has such provinces, whether they be West Indians in Birmingham, or Muslims in Macedonia. But the wide internal variations among children and their educational performance in many countries throw into question the value of aggregated data on the country level. Educational planners need to know the shape of the distributions of performance and the ways in which that shape is rooted in the social fabric and history of a given society. I suspect that in many advanced industrial societies the distributions of educational achievement are bimodal, one mode representing the larger part of the society, which is, in fact, genuinely integrated into its advanced institutions, the other mode representing the preindustrial sector of the population, either the remaining part of the peasant population that is still at the subsistence or near-subsistence level or immigrants from backward or developing countries who, though workers in modern industrial plants, retain a preindustrial culture that is a major handicap to their own children's achievement in the host country's schools. If that is the case, then an analysis of the mean performance of children in those countries obscures and distorts the quite different patterns of performance of the "advanced" and "traditional" parts of the population. If quantitative data on achievement can be organized around these important nationality, ethnic, or regional groups, then we can begin to understand the shape of the whole distribution and the performance of subgroups within the population, in part by reference to the special characteristics and history of the society and its component parts.

This observation is, to me, important, for I cannot be as sure as Husén that the comprehensive principle is necessarily right for a given society without knowing much more about the nature of its population and the range of variability in school performance among major groups within that population. Comprehensive schooling may, in fact, be an educational form that either reflects a high degree of homogeneity in a population, as in Sweden, or is aimed at achieving that homogeneity, as in the United States. But I think that we are all now more sensitive both to group and individual differences among children and more inclined to shape educational forms to accommodate those differences. Comprehensive schooling may be able in principle to provide the wide range of different educational strategies appropriate to a diverse population, but I think it is less likely to be able to do that in practice than where the system itself is structurally more internally differentiated.

Educational policies almost always involve dilemmas. For example, to increase educational diversity is probably also to increase educational inequality. Similarly, to strengthen student and parental choice in education is also likely to strengthen the school's role in transmitting parental status to the children. On the other hand, the use of state education for reducing social inequalities, for equalizing the opportunities and achievements of various groups, may require a high degree of state intervention. It may, for example, abolish the freedom of parents to purchase private education for their children. We need to know more about the costs of our policy choices, for example, the cost of reducing diversity, or of local autonomy, both to students of various kinds and to the climate of freedom in the society at large. Husén's austere definition of comprehensive education implies a high degree of coercion, of central state control, and of standardization, or at least is likely to lead to a suspicion of diversity as a hidden form of educational inequality. If that is the case, then the increasingly diverse society of the future may find the standardized forms of comprehensive education no great service, but a positive hindrance to its total development and to the development of its several parts.

I think there is general agreement that in higher education we want a wide diversity of provisions to reflect the equally wide range of needs and interests that characterize the economies and populations of advanced industrial societies. And systems marked by standard forms of higher education may not serve that diversity as well as systems that comprehend highly diverse forms, from elite research universities, to technological institutions, to various forms of universal access and adult education. But that principle may hold true for secondary education as well.

Moreover, even the principle of prolonged retention in formal education is not now as unquestioned as it was when the main problem was to create a genuine system of secondary education for all. Colemen and his colleagues have recently urged more serious attention in the United States to alternatives to full-time schooling for some proportion of our youth of secondary school age.[3] We may be able to challenge the comprehensive principle more easily when we divorce it from the principle of retentivity.

Finally, Emerson says somewhere that "the health of the eye needs a horizon." And, on the horizon, the creation of structures for permanent education and lifelong learning may have profound consequences for our assumptions about what has to be learned through formal schooling before the age of sixteen or seventeen. There is, in much of the writing that has emerged from the IEA studies thus far, a sense of the older assumptions about formal schooling as a unique opportunity for youngsters before they enter the job market. But I know that Husén shares with me a strong interest in new forms of lifelong learning. A major question, for Sweden, for the United States, and for other industrial societies, is: what are the implications of emerging developments in adult higher education for the assumptions and policies underlying the highly retentive comprehensive school system that Husén so warmly supports?

Notes

1. See, for example, Torsten Husén, "Educational Structure and the Development of Ability," in *Ability and Educational Opportunity*, ed. A. H. Halsey (Paris: Organization for Economic Cooperation and Development, 1961).

2. Martin Trow, "Two Problems in American Secondary Education," in *Social Problems*, ed. Howard Becker (New York: John Wiley, 1966).

3. *Youth: Transition to Adulthood*, Report of the Panel on Youth, President's Science Advisory Committee (Chicago: University of Chicago Press, 1974).

6. Implications of the IEA Studies for Educational Planning with Respect to Organization and Resource Allocation

John Vaizey

In order to approach the problem that has been posed, it is necessary to traverse a small sector of economic theory. Over a decade ago the academic world was warned that if it approached the study of the economics of education by the neoclassical route it would end up by discovering exceedingly little that was of value and possibly even by discrediting the relevance of economics as a discipline in the study of educational problems. This has indeed happened, and the preoccupation with rate of return, which arose from certain views of the nature of capital and the attribution of the income distribution to various factors of production, including privately owned capital, has indeed led to the impasse that was spoken of earlier. The alternative approach, which was largely concerned with establishing the natural history of the economics of education and its connection with modern economic theory by studying the links between the structure of physical capital and the skills and attitudes of the population, has made considerable headway, however, and significant advances have been made whose relevance to the present discussion is great.

This preliminary is necessary since it poses a central question for those considering the place of education in modern society and has relevance to a recent series of comments concerned with the decline of the centrality of economics as the social science discipline that has been concerned with analyzing recent developments in educational theory and practice in connection with planning and administration. As I never held the view that this centrality was necessarily the chief characteristic of the contemporary study of education in this context, I am not particularly surprised by the conclusion. But I think it is unfair to the more thriving schools of economics to saddle them with the view that should be attached only to the neoclassical school, though it is true that the neoclassical school has been particularly dominant in the United States, and consequently (from the very size of that country) has attracted some notoriety.

What has been said of economics would, I think, also apply to other social science disciplines, notably psychology, and in particular to individual psychological testing and measurement. It is for this reason that I would wish to argue that the main classical tradition in economics retains its validity and has indeed much to say about the observations that are reported in the IEA study. This massive study raises major questions that deserve a serious answer from those who are in the mainstream of their disciplines.

Though I have only read three volumes of this study (those dealing with science, literature, and reading), I feel it necessary to begin this paper with a tribute to the enterprise whose results they embody. The original conception of this study was so heroic, the thoroughness with which it has been carried out has been so admirable, and the results are so fascinating that any other scholar, particularly one drawn from a neighboring discipline that faces many similar methodological and ideological problems, must express his gratitude to Professor Husén and his colleagues for the immense amount of pioneering work they have undertaken. It will be many years before the results of this work are fully incorporated in our understanding of social life, particularly its educational aspects; above all, it will be a long time before the methodological implications are fully absorbed.

It follows that the thoughts I present are necessarily preliminary ideas that I shall wish to modify almost immediately and certainly amend drastically in the long run. My present comments should, therefore, be interpreted with caution, since they are very much first impressions.

Perhaps I may begin by recalling that this is a massive survey, undertaken in many countries, of educational achievements in six major fields, and that it follows a survey of mathematics that was not identical, but was similar in conception. That is to say, there is now a multinational study of seven major aspects of the curriculum, conducted by professional educationists. In most countries outside the United States the notion of a professional educationist is a recent one, and it may well be important to remember that their ranks have been largely filled by recruits from particular kinds of psychology and that the history of their discipline has been heavily weighted by the problems of assessment and testing, first of individual children and then of groups. A similar study, using similar funds, that was conducted by social anthropologists or teachers who are specialists in the disciplines assessed in their school context in this study might well have taken a completely different form and consequently have led to different conclusions.

I establish this point at the present stage of my argument because at numerous points in the texts it is asserted that the fundamental reason for the study was to assess the "productivity" of the education system. The first question, therefore, that someone drawn from my discipline is bound to ask is: in what sense is the series of results of the study to be interpreted as an indicator (or a series of indicators) of the "output" of the education systems of the countries concerned? I have alluded in my other work to the considerable danger of incorporating uncritically the results of other sciences in economic analysis, a proposition that may well be generalized to all fields of human knowledge. Because many of the people who have studied the economics of education have been concerned with understanding and interpreting the data thrown up by other studies in order to arrive at a notion of output and to assess productivity, it follows that we have to pay particular attention to this problem here.

One of the major examples that could be given of this is economics itself, and the studies of people who call themselves economists in the field of education have been incorporated with undue simplicity into the work of other specialists. I shall revert to this topic in detail at the end of this chapter, but I feel it necessary at this time to point out that I am no less guilty in this respect than others.

After carefully reading the work presently before us, I find that a number of major points emerge that deserve the fullest consideration

if we are concerned with the organization of education and the
allocation of resources, both within education and to education as a
whole. They reinforce a considerable amount of other evidence that
has been drawn from studies such as those of Jencks and from the
Coleman and Plowden Reports, which do suggest that some major
reappraisal of the organization and structure of the education
system, together with the mechanism for the allocation of resources,
may well deserve further study and consideration. First, however, I
want to present some caveats.

Emphasis is laid upon the importance of formal and nonformal
education in reinforcing learning. It seems that in areas of the curriculum that concern children's immediate experience of life, the
nonformal aspects of education play a particularly important part. It
might be supposed, for example, that children who live in mountain-
ous country would take more naturally to mountaineering as a physical activity than children living in large cities, and similarly, we are
told, particularly in the volume on science, that living in a highly
technological society predisposes children to some understanding of
the nature of the way in which technology and the basic sciences
that underlie it affected their lives. This suggests that in all areas of
the curriculum, amounting in total to the whole educational system,
attention should be paid particularly to the distinction between
formal and nonformal education. This, indeed, has been the subject
of a recent major study undertaken for the World Bank by Philip
Coombs and his associates, who have made this very point, particularly in reference to the developing countries. It is true, of course,
that another way of looking at the distinction between formal and
nonformal education is to see a distinction drawn in different countries between the nature of curricula and the differences in objectives. It is repeatedly stated in the science volume that there have
been recent attempts made in all countries to update the curricula
and to make them subservient to two major objectives: to provide
firsthand experience with the phenomena being studied; and to introduce an element of original investigation into the study. I am forced
to ask at this stage whether or not, despite the exhaustiveness of the
taxonomy of educational objectives that has been adduced by Bloom
and other writers, we have sufficiently considered the degree to
which the education system in each society plays a role that is idio-
syncratic to that society and that might best be investigated by some

form of structuralist anthropological series of tools, which would throw the whole notion of an agreed taxonomy running across cultures into some different light.

It is also important, in taking note of the findings of the study, that we draw special attention to the limitations of the data, particularly because the technical volumes are not available at this stage. Despite the breadth of the study and the depth with which it was carried out, the number of children and teachers surveyed in each nation was comparatively limited. Thus the generalizations drawn from the data may well need to be examined further, particularly when, as appears to be the case in Germany, large elements of the educational system were not included in the survey. The survey in Germany, for example, excluded the technological institutes, and in England the whole network of further education was omitted.

Thus, when we come to answer such questions as those raised by the science study (At what stage can schools first determine which students will be scientists and technologists? How should they be taught? What relationship should this teaching have to the general teaching of science to nonspecialists?), we must realize that the IEA data are not likely to provide a clear answer except within a comparatively narrow conceptual framework. Though this "narrowness" of framework is, of course, considerably broader than any that has hitherto existed, it is not as wide as the framework demanded by specialists in resource allocation in order that they might make some rational (although the word itself is open to further debate and study) division of resources among alternative ends.

I have put forth a sufficient number of objections. It is now time to move forward into some tentative hypotheses about the nature of the likely conclusions that might be drawn.

There is, however, a major prior question: how much should education be regarded as a compensation for forces acting outside the educational system? This is, in a sense, a false question since it poses some sort of opposition between education on the one hand and the rest of society on the other, but within that general area it is fairly easy to see what is implicit in the notion. Science is an important example because of the wide (though not universal) agreement that it is crucial to the understanding of the modern world and therefore is directly related to economic and social change and development.

We are thus faced with the undoubted fact that boys perform

better in science than girls. The conclusion could be drawn either that science education should be concentrated on boys, or, alternatively, that urgent steps should be taken to overcome the apparent distaste that girls have for science. A partial answer to such a question, crudely expressed, might well be that there is some connection between social background that is as important as, or is related to, the differences in sex. This view could be reinforced by the evidence which tended to suggest that interest in science was related in some way to the availability of science teaching. All the studies seem to suggest that the effects of social background, particularly of parental interest and parental occupation, are among the more dominant elements determining whether or not a child "succeeds" in school. It is only after social background has been taken into account that the question of the superiority of teaching by one mode or another, or by one teacher trained in one way or another, can be discussed at all sensibly.

A related issue is the shape and structure of the educational system. If it were decided that the overall aim of education in a particular community were to produce more rather than less science, then one of two conclusions might be drawn: first, that lavish resources should be devoted to all children in the expectation that some would develop while many would not; or, second, that the more precise the selection at an early date, the more the resources could be concentrated on those likely to succeed, with the net result that resources would be allocated more rationally and economically. Clearly, however, what is true for one subject cannot be true for all. The arguments given for science are not the same as for, say, modern languages. But if the community were to accept the narrower second conclusion, the net result would be a decision that education in science should not be provided at all for the less highly motivated children (in this case, those drawn largely from groups of low social origin and suffering from other degrees of cultural and social deprivation).

The school has increasing effects on science learning, effects that become more apparent with age. A subtle analysis of differences in the structures of the school in relation to family and social background might be able to explain many of the results that so far appear inexplicable. These factors must surely explain sex differences in learning, unless further research shows some innate differences in the cast of mind of girls and boys about particular disciplines, which seems improbable.

Those who would assert that the findings in the science study are perfectly compatible with a rational view of the likelihood of the students getting a job related in some way to achievement in science, and those who are unlikely to get such jobs (notably girls and students from less affluent homes) would not pay particular attention to this study. The results appear to suggest that the behavior of the families and their offspring was in this particular context "rational" (an argument to which I shall allude further at the end of this chapter), and to that degree the results might have been known a priori.

In a sense this argument is confirmed by the literature study, which states the case even more strongly: "in the aggregate, therefore, the differences between high achieving and low achieving schools are explained by the culture that they serve." That is put very wisely. The author of the study emphasizes, however, that an assertion of such all-embracing and strong character requires a study of the past and future of the pupils in relation to the changes in values with which the study of literature is particularly meant to be associated. Since the study of literature is not in any direct sense related to future earning power (although the highest proportion of those who come out of the educational system with a qualification are going to be teachers, and for them the study of literature is likely to be a matter of important professional attainment), this result may well be qualified in the same sense in which the result of the science study has been qualified.

The overwhelming importance of socioeconomic backgrounds, however, reinforces the findings of the science study and of the mathematics study undertaken earlier. It suggests that direct action in the socioeconomic sphere should, perhaps, be the first and major priority of any kind of educational reform, although it is important to remember that after this variable has been taken into consideration the type of school and the type of program are themselves important.

The literature study is particularly interesting because it demonstrates the extent to which the responses to literature and presumably, by parallel reasoning, to other affective parts of the curriculum are learned responses, which are the direct result of different styles of educational experience. How far these styles are consciously determined or are cumulative, historic cultural modes needs further exploration. Other studies seem to indicate that these modes of learning are not consciously introduced into the schools, but are the result of social change over lengthy periods.

Since a crucial question concerns the degree to which the schools are effective in giving pupils the tools with which to make sense of the world, clearly the reading comprehension study is fundamental. Here there are major differences between countries, particularly between the developed and the developing countries, indicating once more the importance of the general social context in which education operates. Within the developed countries, furthermore, the socioeconomic origin of students is of fundamental importance; this is reinforced where the schools are socially homogeneous.

As usual, the information about the schools tends to conflict. There is no close relationship between achievement and any of the variables over which administrators have effective control, notably the school organizational program, training of teachers, size of class, specialist teachers, availability of special materials. Further and more detailed studies of schools on an anthropological basis would, perhaps, yield a different set of answers, but at the moment this study tends to reinforce the Coleman and Plowden findings, which suggested the same lack of close relationship between achievement and variables over which administrators have some direct control.

The relationship among the three studies tends to suggest some paradigm of the output of the educational system. There is, of course, a fairly close correlation between science and reading comprehension and between reading comprehension and literature, though the latter is not as close as the former. This suggests that there are variables at work within the schools that could be identified more closely and then could help allocate pupils among different programs. Even more important, however, it suggests a sensible answer to the question posed earlier in this chapter: would a reorganization of resources lead to their more efficient and productive use than is presently the case? The answer must, of course, be positive. One should keep in mind, though, that as the students get older reading comprehension becomes a less valuable predictor, presumably because at a certain point reading skill can be only marginally improved.

Incidentally, it is somewhat erroneous to regard excellence in literature and excellence in science as competing at the higher end of the secondary school in England. Perhaps what is intended to be said is that some schools attract the scientifically gifted and teach them well, while others teach those gifted in languages and teach them well. This does not, however, allow sufficiently for the degree of specialization within the school, and it has tended to exaggerate, as far as I understand the statistical procedures followed, the differences that are revealed.

Economists are forced to conclude, therefore, that the results so far reinforce earlier studies, which tended both to reduce the importance of the school compared to the home and to leave unanswered some of the crucial questions that require answers if a new form of policy for the allocation of resources is to be pursued. But one must ask whether this initial requirement is in itself sensible or rational, and this is where I turn directly to the whole question of the economics of education.

In a recent book, *The Political Economy of Education*,[1] my colleagues and I argued that the boom in the economics of education that has taken place during the last ten years has been largely misguided since it was based upon a form of economics that is in itself of dubious intellectual caliber and that is rapidly being abandoned. This form of economics rests upon the assumptions that there are limited resources that are best allocated by some form of price mechanism; that to each of the major factors in production (notably labor and capital) there is a return; that the optimum allocation of resources is achieved when the marginal rate of return to be derived from an additional input of either labor or capital is equal; and that the purpose of policy must be to create conditions in which something analogous to the price system is functioning, whether or not the price system is actually operating in a normal free market, laissez-faire sense. The fundamental concept used to explain income differentials has been the notion of human capital, that is to say each person is viewed as a machine to whom returns are paid in exactly the same way as in a capitalist society they are paid to the owners of physical machines.

My colleagues and I have argued, with growing support, that this view of the functioning of the economy is incorrect in itself, since it leaves unexplained the notion of capital and gives an inconclusive answer to the question as to what determines prices in the absence of an independently set rate of profit. This debate, which is as old as the science of political economy itself, remains in our view unresolved because the questions are themselves inherently not resolvable, since they are concerned with the opposition of particular interests. In our view, too, the distribution of incomes, though affected by relative scarcities of different types of labor, is fundamentally determined outside the economic system; we think this view is strongly reinforced by the evidence that through time the distribution of incomes varies little. We doubt that major differences in income can be explained by a notion such as human capital, which is highly ambiguous and to which rates of return can only be allocated by separating out from the analysis all those forces which do in fact affect the distribution of income, notably social origin and sex. Our point of view about the nature of economics is a simpler one and might seem to the outsider who has not specialized in the discipline more commonsensical. It is that the explanation of the rate of growth and of change of economies is directly related to the accumulation of physical capital embodying new technologies, that these new technologies call forth from the population differing combinations of skills, that a large part of the function of the educational system is to produce these skills, and that at the same time the major function of the educational system can be directed to the sustaining or the gradual changing of the attitudes of the population toward themselves and their lives, both at work and at leisure.

In such circumstances to ask whether one wishes to improve productivity in education is to ask a question that is in one sense paradoxical, since clearly if there are two courses of action open, the one of which is quick and effective and the other of which is long and ineffective, there can be no doubt about the answer. The purpose of education, on the other hand, is to enable people to lead lives, both at present and in the future, that are satisfying to themselves and to the community in which they live. To attempt to improve productivity in education "on the cheap" may run completely counter to the notion of what is a satisfactory life. The kind of criticism that has frequently been made of economics is in our view wholly compatible with the kind of economics that we ourselves teach and that our work is directed to furthering. It will be found most effectively presented in such outstanding books as Joan

Robinson's *Economic Heresies*, Maurice Dobb's *Theories of Value and Distribution Since Adam Smith*, and Geoffrey C. Harcourt's *Some Cambridge Controversies in the Theory of Capital*.[2] We therefore earnestly beseech our colleagues from other disciplines not to assume that what they may have read in the press concerning the rate of return is the last word in economics. It is far from being the last word. We feel that our own particular approach is likely to prove more fruitful; it also reduces the urgency of the question as to whether or not one particular course of action is more efficient than another. It does not, however, reduce the urgency of one large question: what is the relevance of the education system to the good life? As we understand it, the work reported in the IEA studies gives us our best hope of answering this kind of question.

Notes

1. John Vaizey *et al.*, *The Political Economy of Education* (London: Duckworth, 1972).
2. Joan Robinson, *Economic Heresies: Some Old-Fashioned Questions in Economic Theory* (New York: Basic Books, 1971); Maurice H. Dobb, *Theories of Value and Distribution Since Adam Smith: Ideology and Economic Theory* (Cambridge, Eng.: Cambridge University Press, 1973); Geoffrey C. Harcourt, *Some Cambridge Controversies in the Theory of Capital* (Cambridge, Eng.: Cambridge University Press, 1972).

Commentary I

Jacques Hallak

I would first like to join Professor Vaizey and others who have expressed their admiration for the extraordinary research undertaken by the IEA. While the three volumes already available and the others to come later make a unique contribution in this field, they represent only a small amount of what can potentially be accomplished with the help of the vast and unique stock of accumulated data.

It is appropriate to deal separately with two different though related aspects: the general allocation of resources; and the problems of organization of the use of resources within educational systems.

Professor Vaizey expresses the view that the crucial question for economists is not necessarily that of the general allocation of resources, as explained by the theory of human capital, which essentially relates the distribution of income to the levels of education attained. The IEA studies reinforce this view to the extent that they show that Block 1 is generally a much more important predictor of educational achievement than school variables. "Home background and social origin" (which are included in Block 1) have both a direct and indirect effect on the distribution of income. The effect is direct to the extent that distribution of income is determined to a large extent by social origin; it is indirect because Block 1 is a major determinant of educational performance, which has some consequences on the distribution of income.

Two comments are in order here. First, there is a difference between school-oriented subjects and nonschool-oriented subjects, in the sense that Block 3 is much more powerful as a predictor in "sciences" and "languages" than in "literature" and "reading." In the case of school-oriented subjects, there is still considerable variance between schools that can be explained by variables other than those included in Block 1. Second, it is important to recall that variables in Block 1 are not limited to home background and social origins since sex and age are included (except for French and English). It would, therefore, be misleading to equate variables in Block 1 with "home background and social origins" in the interpretation of the results of the IEA investigations. There are, admittedly, links between the attitudes of the sexes before education and from the sociocultural milieu, but age is so related to the duration of schooling that by including it in Block 1 one can never be sure that the "effectiveness of the education provided by the school is assessed by what is achieved after allowance has been made for the nature of the community in which the school is operating." I believe, therefore, that it is useful to discuss this issue in the context of the role of formal and nonformal education in school achievement.[1] I would suspect that if nonformal education were separated as a predictor of school achievement, Block 1 would have a smaller ability to account for the variance. Block 1 includes, for example, father's education, mother's education, father's occupation, size of family, and two variables that can be judged as indicators of nonformal educational environment: number of books in the home and use of a dictionary in the home.[2] As was pointed out by the authors of Volume I:

> It is frequently assumed that because the teaching and learning of Science is formally prescribed in schools, the knowledge and understanding of Science possessed by the students is solely the outcome of the work of the schools. Little reflection is required to realize that this is not so. From their parents and friends, newspapers, books, television and radio, students, particularly those in western countries, are exposed to extensive discussion on recent developments in Science, on environmental issues, as well as on important scientific ideas and principles. Consequently, at least part of the achievement in Science of the students has been acquired from these less formal sources as well as from more formal learning in schools. The contributions of the mass media and informal opportunities for learning Science are difficult to assess, but are nevertheless substantial and not to be overlooked.[3]

In his chapter Professor Vaizey quite rightly suggests that "in all areas of the curriculum, amounting in total to the whole educational system, attention should be paid particularly to the distinction between formal and nonformal education." If this is acceptable, then one might wonder if in imputing such a large portion of the variance of school achievement to Block 1, one is not overweighting "home background and social origins" by, first, confusing formal and nonformal education in assessing school achievement, and second, ignoring the close relationship between age and duration of schooling. Because of the importance and the generality of the findings of the IEA studies, it might be useful to design a method for separating, from the stock of input variables, what should normally be related to nonformal education exposure. From the content of "International Studies in Evaluation," Volumes I, II, and III, it appears that it would be possible to regroup the variables in such a way that a composite index called "Nonformal Education Exposure" could be identified. It would include:

from Block 1: Reading resources at home and/or
Use of dictionary and/or
Magazines in home and/or
Books in home and so forth
from Block 4: Hours reading for pleasure and/or
Hours per week spent watching television and/or

Reading science (that is, reading science fiction,
articles in newspapers, viewing scientific television
programs) and/or
Reading about sports and so forth

In consequence, there would be five groups of variables:

1. Block 1 revised
2. Nonformal educational exposure
3. Types of school
4. Methods of teaching
5. Kindred variables.

I am not sure whether this can be done (with due care to the problem of asymmetry raised by other participants). If it is possible, it would help to improve the precision of the relationship among the nature of curricula, the educational objectives, and the school inputs.

Thus there is much left to be discovered about interactions of nonschool effects (including home and social background) with school effects and educational achievement. This leads me to the second topic of the paper.

I presume that Vaizey would agree that, especially within the context of countries with limited resources, economists and educational planners are also interested in other aspects relating to resource allocation within the educational system. The following questions are particularly relevant in this respect: What school factors are the most determinant of effectiveness and therefore deserving of financial support? What school factors seem less essential and might represent areas for introducing economies? How much would it cost to increase pupil performance and reduce grade repetition and dropouts, and would it be preferable to do so by improving the level of training of teachers, the value of pupil-teacher ratios, and so on?

In this respect, while it is true that the IEA studies have contributed much to an understanding of the relationship between school input and educational achievement, it is quite clear that, if we omit the role of Block 1 variables, the other results are neither general among countries nor stable among disciplines. For example, the study on reading comprehension concludes:

In general, the factors that it was possible to identify in the school are at best minimally related to reading achievement, and a relationship that is found in any country rarely appears consistently in the others. Even the variables that one might anticipate a priori would be predictors of achievement do not tend to hold up. For example, indicators of training of teachers in the teaching of reading, of size of class, and of availability of specialist teachers in the school all turn out to have either no relationship to reading achievement or a relationship the reverse of what one might anticipate. Thus, the presence of remedial teachers in a school and efforts to individualize teaching by grouping within a class or giving individual instruction to students have, if anything, a negative relationship to measured reading ability.[4]

Nonetheless, in the case of science, English, and literature, where school variables differ and hence are important in terms of resource allocation policy, it appears that they explain between one-quarter and one-third of the total variance. This means that even with the cross-national approach followed by the IEA, it is advisable to examine possibilities for regrouping variables into different blocks leading to stable estimates. Incorporating cost estimates (some of which would be available in the IEA data bank) can help to initiate input-output analysis or cost-effectiveness analysis, which is useful for resource management in education. To give more precise answers to the questions raised above, however, cross-national approaches should be supplemented by parallel analyses for each country. There are two reasons for advocating such parallel studies. On the one hand, out of 200 input variables originally listed by the IEA, several have been omitted in the cross-national investigation, when their partial correlation was judged to be low; it is difficult to assume that all the input variables that were omitted have very low value as predictors in each country. On the other hand, the cross-national approach has led to eliminating some output variables with the result, "in the case of earth sciences, for example, of putting at some disadvantage those countries which include earth sciences in their curricula, when between country comparisons in achievement are made."[5] Thus the advantage of parallel studies is to take into account most relevant output and input variables for each country; it is not certain that the findings in one country should necessarily be replicated in others. This is a hypothesis that is worth testing, as it may lead to better understanding of effective practices and organizational characteristics of the schools in the various countries.

Notes

1. Nonformal education is used here in the sense of exposure to education outside any organized school system, mainly at home.

2. The problem is that father's education as well as mother's education also determines strongly the exposure of the pupils to nonformal education.

3. L. C. Comber and John P. Keeves, *Science Education in Nineteen Countries: An Empirical Study*, International Studies in Evaluation, Vol. I (New York: John Wiley; Stockholm: Almqvist & Wiksell, 1973), 234.

4. Robert L. Thorndike, *Reading Comprehension Education in Fifteen Countries: An Empirical Study*, International Studies in Evaluation, Vol. III (New York: John Wiley; Stockholm: Almqvist & Wiksell, 1973), 178.

5. Comber and Keeves, *op. cit.*, 26.

Commentary II

Angus Maddison

The IEA studies of secondary school achievement in mathematics and six other subjects will help transform the study of comparative education. This type of material makes it possible to move from descriptive to normative comparisons of educational performance and permits identification of more effective policy options. One must distinguish, however, between the great mound of research material that has been assembled and the use made of it so far in the published reports, of which only the studies on mathematics, reading, literature, and science are yet available. Critical scrutiny of these reports can help indicate ways in which the existing material can be better exploited and can show how to improve the design of future tests. Any outside critic must stand in awe of the enterprise, energy, and ingenuity of the IEA, and, with the work only partly published, he is bound to make some suggestions that are wide of the mark or impossible to fulfill. My own points are presented with due humility and respect.

In my view the existing reports fall short in two ways. The first problem is that the technical description is written for insiders. Some difficult points need more careful explanation, some important problems concerning the data are not discussed, some basic data are omitted, and the description of procedures is often mixed up with analysis of particular issues of policy. The average schoolteacher interested in this field would, therefore, have difficulty in knowing what was done, and a scholar seeking research material will sometimes be forced to use the data tapes for rather elementary things.

The second problem is that the reports deal rather elliptically with questions of policy. There are good diplomatic reasons for not pushing policy conclusions too far at this stage because the general reports will be followed by studies of individual countries, which will be able to formulate policy suggestions in a more operational form than is possible in an international study. One cannot risk losing the goodwill of potential participants in future exercises by premature suggestions concerning policy. When policy questions are tackled, however, they should be stated clearly and examined rigorously; otherwise there is confusion both on the conclusions and the validity of the procedures. A major issue in the study on mathematics, and one that is also a leitmotiv in the six-subject study, is whether "more means worse."

It is puzzling that reports as serious as these should pose an important policy issue in such a telegraphic form. There are really two separate issues: whether a major increase in enrollment ratios (such as all countries have experienced in the past twenty years) is likely to reduce the average performance of those in school because the new entrants will be less bright than the students already enrolled (that is, one is testing the hypothesis of the "restricted pool of talent" advocated by those who opposed the expansion of British higher education as proposed in the Robbins Report); and whether a switch from selective to nonselective schools will have harmful effects on the learning processes of bright students (a position advocated by opponents of comprehensive education). The IEA studies contain material that can illuminate both issues, but the first is more amenable to general cross-country conclusions, while the second needs much more analysis on a level of individual countries because a wider range of policy options have been employed. There are places in the reports, however, where it seems to be suggested that if one deals with the first issue he has also dealt with the second. If the second problem is to be treated seriously, outside evidence is needed to supplement that gathered from the studies, and it will be necessary to consider some practical issues in detail, for example, how fast a switch can be made from a selective to a nonselective system without reducing quality. But this is not done, mainly I suspect because the authors tend to treat the policy issues as illustrations of what can be done with the data rather than tackling the issues themselves in a satisfactory way. The "more means worse" slogan does not really cover the second issue and is not the best way to summarize the first issue. Husén states the first problem in a more sophisticated and less defensive form in Chapter 5, where he produces rough estimates of average achievement levels of whole populations of a given age to supplement the comparison restricted to those in school. This is a more useful statement of the issue for those interested in the likely impact of extending school facilities to the whole society.

I would conclude therefore that the published reports need to be supplemented by a book containing basic data and a simple, general methodological introduction; and that in future studies issues of policy should be more clearly formulated. I would also suggest that some other approaches and issues could be tested; they are outlined in the following paragraphs.

The material available is probably broad enough to provide an aggregate picture of cognitive achievement in different systems. The study itself claims that it covers "practically all the principal academic subjects in the secondary curriculum apart from the classical languages." It is surprising, therefore, that the very idea of "cognitive Olympics" is so brusquely rejected. Comparative standings can be very useful in policy analysis, and people will construct them whether you want them or not. It is better to compile them yourself and explain the difficulties in interpreting them rather than leaving the job to outsiders. At the moment the reports do not discuss some of the important problems that arise in this context, and most of them could be solved without further surveys. These problems are:

1. Finding appropriate weights to aggregate the results in different fields.

2. Assessing whether the results in different fields are compatible; for example, the mathematics study dealt with thirteen-year-olds, the others with fourteen-year-olds. What correction factors are needed to solve this problem?

3. Determining how representative the tests are of the whole field of instruction; for example, history and geography are not covered, and the literature tests are in large part an advanced form of testing for reading knowledge with many aspects of literature excluded. The use of multiple-choice questions means that higher cognitive skills are

not well tested, and it could also be argued that, in some countries, the tests may not be fair in relation to what is contained in the curriculum. I do not know how important these criticisms might be, but if they are important, improvements could be made in future tests or correction coefficients applied to present results. There is also the problem that not all subjects were tested in all countries. There was, in fact, no country that tested all target populations in all subjects. Can one use some subjects as rough proxies for others? How many countries can be safely put in the table of comparative standings?

4. Assessing whether the rank order would have been substantially affected by more difficult or easier questions. Would there have been larger variations between countries in the performance of the top 1 to 9 percent if the questions had been more difficult? Would there have been a smaller difference between developed and developing countries if tests had been easier? Would it have been better to set different standards for developed and developing countries in order to analyze variance better in the latter and then link the results via anchor items?

5. Determining the accuracy of the estimates of retentivity rates (that is, the measures of the proportion of population in school at a specific age). We have spent several months trying to establish such figures on a comparable basis for countries in the Organization for Economic Cooperation and Development, and the difficulties have been substantial. For some countries it was not possible to make estimates. The main problem arises with older pupils who may be spread over several different kinds of full-time school, and a fair proportion of whom are engaged in part-time study. It is not enough to say that 9 percent of Germans are in school at age nineteen years, three months. This presumably means the average for males and females in full-time formal secondary schooling, but what percent were in part-time schooling or had entered higher education? This is an area that must be explored further if one is to make rough estimates, as Husén does, of the cognitive achievements of whole populations. In future studies one could perhaps hope for some attempt to measure directly the achievement levels of those not in school; one might also ask these people how much schooling they have had.

6. Taking account of the wide range of ages in Population IV. In

India the science pupils were sixteen years and ten months on the average, whereas in Finland the average age was nineteen years and eleven months. In future studies it is desirable to measure achievement at a single year of age, whether the students are in secondary school or in higher education. This would permit more effective analysis of the incremental value of educational systems and aid in the consideration of policy options concerning initial and terminal ages for education.

In order to illuminate the importance of educational resource inputs it is desirable to mention the following points.

One major input is student time. The study by Passow and others shows theoretical cumulated school hours per pupil over his whole school career prior to testing.[1] This is useful information which does not appear in the other reports. Some adjustment should be made for truancy and sickness rates which must be much higher in developing than in developed countries. One needs to determine whether performance is sensitive to the number of hours per year of education. If not, what scope is there for economies of resources by double-shift teaching?

More attention could be devoted to the phasing of the inputs of students' time and the relative costs of different options. The most explicit discussion of this is in Postlethwaite's analysis of the mathematics study where he concluded that starting school at age five had no advantage over starting at age six, but that a start at age seven led to poorer performance at age thirteen. Do the same conclusions hold for terminal secondary students? The six-subject studies do not raise the issue even though there is a wide dispersion (almost three years) in the average age of terminal secondary students. There should be some discussion of the costs of prolonging secondary education to the extent that is done in Scandinavia. More explicit consideration of the cognitive impact (if any) of preprimary education could be helpful. Governments are now spending a good deal on this, and there is need to establish whether there is any cognitive return. One could easily ask the pupils being tested how much preprimary education they have had.

The question of student-teacher ratios is very important, but the reports do not show data on class size or proportion of time the teacher actually spends on teaching. One gets the impression that class size is not considered to have much impact on performance, which, if correct, would be of major significance in relation to policy. According to Postlethwaite's reporting, however, the student-teacher ratio ranged from fourteen to twenty-two in the developed countries, but from twenty-four to seventy-two in the developing world. What impact does this wide variation have on performance? The differential might be more interesting than lesser variations in class size within the developed world. It might also be the case that class size is more important in some fields and at some ages than at others; these factors are also important for policy.

Apart from teachers, other personnel inputs are important, and data on these were apparently collected, but not reported in the published studies. I am not only referring to "ancillary" personnel but to all nonteaching personnel inputs. It would be useful to have cumulative information on inputs of teachers and nonteaching personnel so that one could get a rough assessment of the situation concerning student-teacher and auxiliary inputs over the pupil's educational career.

Governments spend much on school buildings and equipment; one would like to know more about the impact of physical facilities on performance. The information is difficult but not impossible to collect in comparable form, and it would be interesting to have a short complementary study on this. Here again cumulative as well as current experience must be kept in mind; the difference in the physical environment for terminal secondary students in India and the United States will probably be smaller than their cumulative experience. There are considerable difficulties in securing comparable financial data on educational costs. If the information is to be collected from pupils and teachers, one should concentrate on resource inputs in real terms as described in the preceding points. Financial data can be useful, however, in measuring trade-offs between different types of resource input and in judging claims for teachers' pay. Passow's study indicates that Swedish teachers are paid 2.4 times the average earnings of those employed in the area of manufacturing, whereas in India the relative wage is .8. It is to be hoped that future studies will involve more direct cooperation with national educational authorities who could be asked to prepare the financial and cost data.

A major issue discussed in the six-subject study is the relative importance of the home versus the school. On the whole, the reports give more weight to home variables than to school variables, as was the case with the Coleman study in the United States. Coleman's paper, however, criticizes the IEA techniques for partitioning the contribution of home and school (endorsing to some extent the arguments that Eric Hanushek and J. F. Kain used in criticism of his own study). Coleman suggests that the IEA reports have understated the importance of schooling. Apart from the technical reasons advanced by Coleman, one must doubt if anything definitive can be said about the relative importance of home and school until information is available on the cognitive achievement and background of people in the same age group who are not in school. If the operational significance of the studies for policy is to be increased, future studies should perhaps pay less attention to collecting some of the more vaguely defined home variables and more to accumulating harder information on school inputs that are amenable to public policy. It would also seem desirable to try, at least for some countries, to collect information on parental income—the fundamental home variable amenable to public policy.

The six-subject study has not so far properly exploited the fact that it includes developing as well as developed countries. The performance of the two sets of countries is so different that much could be learned by statistical analysis of them as two dichotomous groups rather than by treating all countries as having the same significance. Consideration of the cognitive gap is rather casual in the reports. The poor performance of Chile, India, and Iran is ascribed to vague cultural influences, mainly to the fact that they have a shorter tradition of formal education. This is somewhat fatalistic in view of the large differences in resources invested per pupil (teachers, auxiliary staff, buildings, and so forth). There should be more discussion of whether easier tests might not have improved the relative performance of these countries and whether there are other factors for which substantial allowance should be made (such as the fact that the Indians in Population IV were so young, the fact that a high proportion of pupils in India and Iran speak a different language at home than in school, the fact that truancy and sickness ratios are higher in developing countries, the fact that English medium schools are excluded in India though they are the normal type of schooling for children from the wealthier families, the fact that average temperature in the classroom was much higher in India and Iran than in other countries). The whole question of the relative performance of developing and developed countries deserves treatment in a separate monograph, preferably by an interdisciplinary team including an economist. This would permit more sophisticated use of background material, such as real income levels or quality of school buildings.

Note

1. A. H. Passow *et al.*, *The National Case Study: An Empirical Comparative Study of Twenty-one Educational Systems* (Stockholm: Almqvist & Wiksell, in press).

Commentary III

Russell G. Davis

The IEA studies, covering as they do the assessment of achievement in up to four age-grade levels, for up to six subject areas, in up to twenty-three countries, represent another heroic effort in the line that comes out of such precursors as the Educational Opportunities Survey, Project Talent, the National Assessment of Educational Progress, other previous IEA international assessments, and the Pennsylvania Study of Quality of Education. The current IEA studies are, in fact, even more heroically cast than their forebears, and they are just as limited in their usefulness in providing an information base for planning and for allocation of resources. Vaizey makes this point in Chapter 6 mainly by dealing gracefully with other points, and Platt makes the point more explicitly by enumerating specific planning and policy issues that the IEA data do not address. Both, however, pay deserved tribute to the studies and their sponsors. I add my tribute gladly for I know that what a planner would really like to demand as an information base for the simplest kind of planning and resource allocation model could not be demanded of the IEA studies in the first place.

From the viewpoint of an educational planner working mainly in developing countries, the ideal information base for national systems planning and resource allocation would include the following:

1. Social, economic, political, and cultural goals translated into observable indicators of the required traits and performance characteristics of citizens, workers, and parents.

2. Data on school structures, programs, and provisions that when interrelated in some describable way with the social, intellectual, and motivational characteristics of learners enhance in some observable way the traits and performance characteristics of citizens, workers, and parents with respect to the indicators mentioned in the first point. It is not necessary to consider nonformal education, whatever that is; I would settle for information on what is wanted out of schools, what learners bring into the schools, and what the schools can do to add something related to what is wanted in the first place. If the order for information cannot be specified any more clearly than this, it seems unreasonable to expect that the IEA study or any similar venture can fill the order.

All the large-scale studies have been useful. The National Assessment of Educational Progress provided normative information that ranged beyond the school groups tested in the IEA studies and tended toward the performance of citizens and workers. The reports I saw, however, did not attempt to trace performance to school programs or student characteristics interacting with programs, and I think the work of the IEA was more useful in this sense. The Pennsylvania Study of Quality Education provided clues to the association between school programs and performance, but stayed within the student world, as did the IEA studies. The Educational Opportunities Survey attempted to relate school achievement to student and school and community characteristics, but it was bound into a cross section of time as the IEA studies were. Project Talent provides, or may when the course has been run and the results analyzed, links over time between school and students, community and citizens, and the world of work and workers, and their traits and performance characteristics, but the connection between these and school programs was difficult for me to follow. None of the studies had good data on cost and resources; hence it is difficult to base decisions concerning resource allocations on them, as is the case with the IEA studies. The IEA has the added dimension of comparison over a wider domain and thus shares the added disability long ago described in the phrase "All Comparisons Limp." If this is so, it is traceable, I feel, to very honorable wounds.

Although, for reasons to be treated briefly later, the IEA provides little data with a direct bearing on planning and allocations decisions, such of the studies as I have seen yield much that is of interest to a planner. Coleman's reparceling of variation attributable to school effects distributed independently of home and school for ten-year-olds in reading and science was particularly interesting when the comparison between Chile and other developed countries was set against the comparison of results for fourteen-year-olds in the same countries and for the same subjects. In the developing countries, partly as an antidote to interpretations of the findings from the Educational Opportunities Survey and partly because of some meager data we have gathered in those countries, we have been establishing a notion we call the "threshold hypothesis." We argue that the relatively weak relationship between school input variables and achievement shown in data on developing countries may reflect the fact that in the developed countries even the meanest provisions are substantially above a threshold where clear relationships might be expected. Or the argument can be tipped upside down, and we can argue that in the developing countries provisions are below (in some cases absent), and thus relationships do appear stronger. We can buttress the argument. In developed countries the weak effect of school inputs when compared with community-school characteristics in predicting variation in achievement is influenced by the crippling and powerful effect of the relative deprivation observed. Since relative deprivation is especially keen in a materialistic country, a powerful argument for the "threshold hypothesis" emerges. We do have some data and hope, with luck, to have some more to confirm the hypothesis. From an allocations standpoint, we have little trouble arguing for placing nearly all resources in primary education, particularly in a situation where it is manifestly underfinanced compared to other aspects of the system whose value is ambiguous. Meanwhile, we try to get more data that will support the argument.

The IEA results also may support an argument we have long been making about the importance of providing books to children through school and neighborhood libraries, and to do so at low cost and in an expendable fashion, thus making it possible for books to be brought into homes. Again we have some evidence of the effect of this type of program in one section of one developing country; thus the argument is not wholly impressionistic or unprincipled. I was shaken by Professor Thorndike's description of the scale used to determine "possession" by the numbers of books in the home: "A. None; B. 1-10; C. 11-25; D. 26-50; and E. 51 or more books." Apart from the problem Thorndike pointed out in the piling up of frequencies in one category, I wondered if a child with a rather hazy memory for numbers, and one small book at issue, might chose category E because of higher status, or category D because of digit preference for the zero in the fifty. In a study of McGinn and Davis[1] we found possession of books in the home highly related to success in school although the questionnaire combined books with other possessions in a composite item. Having cause to reexamine those results in comparison to the IEA, I noted that our item did not ask for numbers of books, but rather kinds of books, and about 50 percent of the books in the homes were described as "school books." We commend these kinds of cross checks to the attention of path analysts everywhere. In the IEA studies it was also interesting that magazines showed a clear relationship to reading comprehension scores, although this relationship did not show clear differences between developing and developed countries.

The IEA studies presented evidence that would enable one to argue for the importance of early childhood education, at least for augmenting the number of preprimary grades or for establishing day-care centers with learning experiences added to the usual custodial or nutritional programs. This evidence will not greatly influence decisions concerning allocations or planning in most developing countries where the need to justify the worth of preprimary education is not so great a problem as is that of the brutally exiguous resources that make it problematical in some cases whether even ten-year-olds can be admitted to the primary grades.

Other findings of the studies point to the need for more explicit and more enduring attention to the development of reading skills, and this implication is useful to file away for program planning purposes. The relationships of teacher education and opportunity to learn in science provide stimulating indications, useful for guiding future plans and allocations decisions, as to whether accompanying cost information provides a basis for comparison of alternative arrangements and provisions. I could go on mentioning indications that interested me, and if my comments sound like the daily journal of a string collector, then so be it, for this is the way such a study should serve the planner, and it does not bother me that it gives scant basis for planning aggregate allocations to large social, educational, and economic goals.

I return to my original statement: it is unreasonable for planners to expect that studies such as those of the IEA will provide a ready-made information base that serves most systems planning and allocations decisions.

First, as a practical planner charged with decisions on allocations, I would like a study to furnish information that would be useful to answer directly and in appropriate terms the kinds of questions that I ask. I would like, in short, answers to the kinds of questions that Platt raises and in the terms in which he raises them: What is the appropriate mixture of cognitive and other learning outcomes in the program? What is the right number of students per teacher? What is the appropriate number of teachers and students per school? What is the necessary support for teachers and students? The problem is that even the most seemingly simple of these questions is not amenable to a straightforward answer at a level of generality sufficient to be of use to a decision maker charged with setting policy and determining resource allocations at the systems level. If there has been one thing over the years that has frustrated the Ministers of Education for whom I have worked it has been my inability to give a straightforward answer to a simple question: what is the appropriate teacher-pupil ratio? This seems to be a reasonable question, and since I want to seem to be a reasonable man, I give an answer. It varies between ten and fifty, depending on circumstances, but though I deliver it in a straightforward fashion, it is not always a straightforward answer. I have been in circumstances where my own honest estimate has ranged from five to one (not five students to a teacher, but five teachers to a student) to a ratio of thousands to one (meaning thousands of students to a teacher on TV). I suggest that there is usually no meaningful single answer to the question, but even if there were one, and I had it, it would not help much in systems planning or allocations decisions.

Planning and allocations decisions for a school system of any size and complexity cannot be based on mere assemblages of information, no matter how precise, accurate, and voluminous the data may be. The information must be marshaled into some format or model that relates the main components of the system. Now if we had the pupil-teacher ratio we could put it in a model of the kind used for determining allocations at the aggregate or systems level. Say it is embedded in the form:

$$a_{11}X_1 + a_{12}X_2 + \dots a_{1n}X_n \leq b_1$$
$$a_{21}X_1 \dots \qquad\qquad\qquad \leq b_2$$
$$\vdots$$
$$a_{m1}X_1 + \dots a_{mn}X_n \qquad\qquad \leq b_n$$

where the b's represent a resource to be allocated (such as numbers and types of teachers), the X's some activity level or output of education (say a student-year of primary schooling), and the a's, the teacher resource per student-year of education (the teacher-pupil ratio). If we knew our resource limits, we could then allocate so as to reach output targets of education within them. If we knew our objectives in comparable terms, which we usually do not, then we could move our various allocations possibilities around a bit, which we usually cannot. Even if we could do so, however, we would probably not affect our allocations decisions, since we are not answering questions in the terms in which they were asked in the first place. For what the Minister of Education (one who cares, that is) would again ask is: "But how did you get the teacher-pupil ratio?"

Just as there are several ratios for any given situation, so there are several answers to a question that cannot honestly be answered in the situation. We could say that we might approximate an answer by a long set of experimental studies in which we considered various combinations of teacher types and numbers in various kinds of teaching-learning situations with various kinds of results. That is a long, expensive, and tedious process that usually gets overtaken by events and change and usually does not produce results that are either timely or general enough to be useful for mortal men and decision makers. Studies such as those of the IEA would, however, be more harmful than useful if they discouraged this kind of continuing research by suggesting that only large and impressive projects can produce timely and useful results through regression analysis applied to cross-section data. I would measure the success of the IEA studies by the number of experimental studies it stimulates; the IEA has, in fact, suggested a few that I would be interested in pursuing, such as analyzing the "opportunity to learn" variable. I would also count against the IEA the number of times experimental studies are neglected by future researchers who hope to pull something off the data tapes by regression analysis applied again and again to the cross section and pasted together with data gathered in some other time and place for another purpose.

To return to the Minister's question, we could also answer that we have a pile of data such as the IEA or similar organizations produce, and we can disaggregate, apply production function analysis, and thus estimate relationships between inputs and outputs. Vaizey criticizes the misalliance of economics and education through the notion of human capital, but my target is smaller and is limited to some of the uses of so-called production function analysis in educational planning.

Regression analysis applied to cross-sectional data to yield "educational production" functions does not provide results that I would use to determine the allocation of resources in a school situation. Quite apart from the more obvious problems of the relevance of the criterion measures used, of the difficulty of associating input units as dealt with in reality with what are described as independent variables in analysis and of the fact that the school inputs are associated with only a part of the criterion variation anyway (all problems that must be dealt with), my own difficulty comes with the discrepancy between a teaching-learning model and a model of analysis that purports to explain the first model sufficiently for a decision maker to predict the future consequences of allocations decisions. What I think I know about the teaching-learning situation is that there is no one combination of antecedents (instructional strategies, resource provisions, and so forth) that holds for all, in the sense that it will produce an effect in a specified direction. It is probably true that there is no combination that produces the same effect for any two learners seemingly in the same situation; it is at least sometimes true that a combination that produces an effect in one direction for one learner produces an opposite effect for another; and a combination that produces an effect on one learner in one time and circumstance may produce a different effect in another time or circumstance. Because "produce" and "effect" are not appropriate in a discussion of regression, "associated with" should be substituted.

When multiple regression analysis is applied in cross section to yield differing slope coefficients, which presumably measure the relationship between changes in the independent or predictor variables with respect to change in the dependent or criterion variable, I have no way of knowing whether the combination that is yielded in these circumstances reflects a relationship that has any meaning in terms of any member of the aggregation for which it is averaged; at least insofar as teaching and learning go. I can discover, if I look into it, where individual i is with respect to the mean on dependent Y and on the independents X_1 and X_2 . . . in combination, but I do not know where i would be on a different combination, only where j is on his particular combination. A different combination of X's might move i up on Y and j down, unless I can think that i learns like j when my learning model seems to suggest otherwise. What we seem to have experimentally is a situation where we cannot vary the treatments but only the subjects and, hence, the criterion. The data in the first place represent an aggregate of less than optimal learning circumstances that are in the case of schooling limited greatly in their variation by conventions. I was struck in the IEA data by the limited range of many of the school effect variables, indicating that schooling is depressingly similar the world over, given minimum resources to get up to a minimal level.

We can avoid some limitations by going to another set of data, or building in the results from another study as a means of structuring the analysis of this set of data. We note that there is some evidence from somewhere that some groups that can be identified by some characteristics perform differently from other groups according to differing combinations of independent variables. We then regroup and try this out on our cross section of data. The ratio of the variance on the comparison between groups to the comparison within groups or partial correlation may indicate that the combinations of inputs relate to the performance of the different groups differently. This is useful, but we also know, or we should, that if we subdivided our groups, perhaps on the basis of yet another study, we would then find differing combinations relating differently to the subgroups.

And so we go on. All the while error intrudes, variables pop in and out of the combinations, criteria shift, betas rise and fall, and finally we do not have a sample of our subgroups. The end result, as it comes somewhere close to reflecting the teaching-learning situation, is that we have a set of input specifications, not necessarily a good set because they are what was in the situation in the first place, and that is a mixed bag, and not even a very useful set in the sense that we cannot allocate resources to them in the form and combination in which we deal with them. And these combinations are related to groups described by characteristics that intersect in an artifice that does not correspond with anything we can deal with in reality.

We could say that we could have dealt with data from a place where things are done right in the first place, but that only tells us what we knew from the outset. The Minister wants to know not how to get favorable results out of the favorable situation, but how to get the best results he can out of the unfavorable ones—for that is what he has to deal with. The answer, if there is one, is that we should probably realize that the cross-section data, such as those of the IEA, provide us some hints on broad scale that may help to guide our experience and intuition and provide some directions for further experiment and testing when we do not trust our experience and intuition. That is enough for a planner to ask.

On the basis of the cross-section analysis, I would not combine regression results with costs and use this combination to allocate resources to some entirely different set of learners in a different time and circumstance. There is also the possibility of collecting data in time series and applying spectral analysis, but we have found that there are some formidable problems in getting enough data points in two series, and autocorrelation is the nature of the situation. Whatever the method of analysis applied, however, the results cannot be plugged into the kind of "allocations" model previously sketched in order to make allocations decisions. The so-called allocations model, when appropriately elaborated and perhaps equipped with an objective function, can be applied to many useful purposes, but not to actual allocations. It can be used pedagogically to give students of planning a clearer notion of the interrelatedness of components of an

educational system (such as enrollment flows and teacher requirements); it can be used to inform policy makers about possible consequences of changes in policy or programs; it can provide broad
hints about bottlenecks in systems; and all of these uses make it
sufficiently worthwhile. The same holds for regression analysis
applied to tracing out broad-scale relationships among schooling
conditions. Since I would not use the numerical results of regression
applied to production function analysis for allocating resources, I
would even less trust the model for determining social policy by the
numbers. My criticism of the possible misuse of the model and
methods, however, is directed at overextended application and over-
blown promise, and not at many instances of proper use. I use regression analysis to provide clues as to possible directions in plans,
policies, and program development. I see much merit in the use of it
in the careful statements by IEA analysts on the data in order to
make relationships within it more perspicuous and suggestive for
educational researchers and practitioners. For planning and resource
allocation I am satisfied with the broad indications of the kind I have
mentioned, especially for the suggestions they provide for follow-up
in experimental studies in situations more nearly akin to teaching
and learning as modeled by those expert in such matters.

Note

1. Noel F. McGinn and Russell Davis, *Build a Mill, Build a City, Build a
School: Industrialization, Urbanization, and Education in Ciudad Guyama*
(Cambridge, Mass.: M.I.T. Press, 1969).